D1545458

WITHDRAWAL

NEW DIRECTIONS FOR ADULT AND CONTINUING EDUCATION

Ralph G. Brockett, *University of Tennessee, Knoxville*
Susan Imel, *Ohio State University*
EDITORS-IN-CHIEF

Alan B. Knox, *University of Wisconsin, Madison*
CONSULTING EDITOR

A Community-Based Approach to Literacy Programs: Taking Learners' Lives into Account

Peggy A. Sissel
University of Arkansas at Little Rock

EDITOR

Number 70, Summer 1996

JOSSEY-BASS PUBLISHERS
San Francisco

A COMMUNITY-BASED APPROACH TO LITERACY PROGRAMS:
TAKING LEARNERS' LIVES INTO ACCOUNT
Peggy A. Sissel (ed.)
New Directions for Adult and Continuing Education, no. 70
Ralph G. Brockett, Susan Imel, Editors-in-Chief
Alan B. Knox, Consulting Editor

Microfilm copies of issues and articles are available in 16mm and 35mm,
as well as microfiche in 105mm, through University Microfilms Inc., 300
North Zeeb Road, Ann Arbor, Michigan 48106-1346.

ISSN 0195-2242   ISBN 0-7879-9867-2

NEW DIRECTIONS FOR ADULT AND CONTINUING EDUCATION is part of The
Jossey-Bass Higher and Adult Education Series and is published quarterly
by Jossey-Bass Inc., Publishers, 350 Sansome Street, San Francisco,
California 94104-1342. Periodicals postage paid at San Francisco,
California, and at additional mailing offices. POSTMASTER: Send address
changes to New Directions for Adult and Continuing Education, Jossey-
Bass Inc., Publishers, 350 Sansome Street, San Francisco, California
94104-1342.

SUBSCRIPTIONS for 1996 cost $50.00 for individuals and $72.00 for institutions, agencies, and libraries.

EDITORIAL CORRESPONDENCE should be sent to the Editor-in-Chief,
Susan Imel, ERIC/ACVE, 1900 Kenny Road, Columbus, Ohio 43210-1090.
E-mail: imel.1@osu.edu.

Cover photograph by Wernher Krutein/PHOTOVAULT © 1990.

TCF   Manufactured in the United States of America on Lyons Falls
      Pathfinder Tradebook. This paper is acid-free and 100 percent
totally chlorine-free.

august 13,2004

CONTENTS

EDITOR'S NOTES

The focus of this sourcebook is to provide adult literacy practitioners in all program settings with critical insights from emerging areas of interest and scholarship as these insights relate to the future needs, concerns, and contexts of literacy programming. Designed to encourage readers to reflect on these emerging areas of thought, this volume provides new examples and perspectives that apply to both program and staff development.

This sourcebook has two main emphases: issues of the future and issues of community. The future-focused approach is apparent in the contributors' many suggestions for program development and change. As Imel (1990) succinctly reminds us, adult educators "must be proactive in guiding the field toward the future they desire" (p. 405). This volume envisions a future of hope and possibility, in which literacy programming is learner centered, participatory, and based in the contexts and concerns of learners both as individuals and as members of communities.

The second emphasis of this sourcebook is that all literacy providers, regardless of orientation, need to embrace a community-based approach that takes into account the reality of learners' lives; incorporates knowledge about learners' context, culture, and community into program practice; and emphasizes learner-centered and participatory approaches to programming (Fingeret and Jurmo, 1989).

Sondra Cuban and Elisabeth Hayes begin the discussion of future needs in Chapter One. Although family literacy programs have developed around the country as a vital new approach to literacy programming, this intergenerational focus has neglected the reality that 90 percent of the parents in these programs are women. Cuban and Hayes explore the ramifications of this fact for curriculum and program development.

Chapter Two, by Elizabeth Peterson, examines the historical and cultural realities and needs of African Americans in literacy programs and explores race and ethnicity in relation to future program concerns. Peterson discusses the emancipatory promise that the acquisition of literacy has traditionally held for the African American community and the need to revisit literacy as a source of hope, strength, and skill building.

Loida Velázquez shares views of the cultural life and educational experiences of migrant workers in Chapter Three. She emphasizes that practitioner recognition of migrants' values and beliefs, cultural and historical background, and past schooling experiences is of vital importance to meeting the learning needs of migrants in English as a Second Language (ESL) and Adult Basic Education (ABE) programs.

Chapter Four examines the experiences of learners and literacy providers working in penal institutions. Authors Waynne Blue James, James Witte, and David Tal-Mason address emerging trends in prison programs and show that

NEW DIRECTIONS FOR ADULT AND CONTINUING EDUCATION, no. 70, Summer 1996 © Jossey-Bass Publishers

learners in these programs can also benefit from learner-centered program approaches that incorporate understandings of inmates as members of communities.

Chapter Five presents a model for developing community among learners, as Mary Beth Bingman, Marie Martin, and Amy Trawick describe their work in a rural Appalachian project designed to incorporate community issues into practitioners' work with ABE learners. By drawing upon a community's accomplishments, hopes, and concerns outside the classroom, teachers and learners can jointly develop meaningful learning experiences.

In Chapter Six, Marcia Drew Hohn and I address the barriers that low literates encounter in accessing health care and health information, examine the rationale for incorporating health materials in literacy programs, and discuss innovative models of implementation. They also address the need to develop connections among learners and between health care and literacy provider systems.

Chapter Seven revisits the wisdom and knowledge of Latin American theorists and practitioners of popular education, wisdom that has long been a source of reflection for North American adult educators. Author Hal Beder shares his experience and insights about building community through popular education in the United States and Canada and provides ways to incorporate popular education into adult education programming.

Chapter Eight, by Susan Lytle, challenges literacy providers to become cognizant not only of the contexts of learners' lives but also of program-setting dynamics that may be promoting or impeding adults' participation and learning. An inquiry-based approach to practice that supports continued reflection and staff development can be important to meeting the range of needs that learners bring to programs.

Finally, in Chapter Nine, I sum up the views and suggestions of the contributors and suggest questions for reflection regarding the future roles of both learners and educators in community-based literacy programming.

The underlying message of this sourcebook is that understanding the context of learners' lives is critical to meeting their learning needs. This volume is intended to serve as a source of reflection for practitioners, program developers, and policy makers. It is my hope that such reflection will promote insightful discussion among staff, volunteers, and funders alike as they work toward meeting the needs of their communities, in whatever contexts they are found.

Peggy A. Sissel
Editor

References

Fingeret, A., and Jurmo, P. (eds.). *Participatory Literacy Education.* New Directions for Adult and Continuing Education, no. 42. San Francisco: Jossey-Bass, 1989.

Imel, S. "Perspectives on the Future." In M. Galbraith (ed.), *Adult Learning Methods.* Malabar, Fla.: Krieger, 1990.

PEGGY A. SISSEL is assistant professor with the Center for Research on Teaching and Learning, College of Education, University of Arkansas at Little Rock, and adjunct assistant professor, Department of Pediatrics, University of Arkansas for Medical Sciences.

What do women participants in family literacy programs want and need? Little attention has been given to these women's dream of an education for themselves as well as their children.

Women in Family Literacy Programs: A Gendered Perspective

Sondra Cuban, Elisabeth Hayes

In a recent survey of dropouts from a family literacy program (Nurss and Singh, 1993), one woman's comment stood out. Asked what she did not learn in the program, she replied, "[I] thought it would be more like school" (p. 7). Others also reported an interest in a more "academic" and businesslike orientation (pp. 4–5). These women were looking for a serious educational opportunity for *themselves,* aside from their children. Family literacy providers need to hear these women's voices and attend to women's educational needs as well as those of their children.

For many low-income women, family literacy programs are meaningful first steps inside the adult education system. Designed specifically for the hardest-to reach, these community-based approaches provide functional literacy skill training in a supportive environment transferable to the home. Although adult female participants make up between 80 to 100 percent of the adults in most programs—due in large part to innovative and integrated programming and recruitment strategies, agency collaborations, aggressive funding efforts, and provision of such services as comprehensive child care—gender is typically an unarticulated topic. Gender-neutral language in much program literature disguises the numbers and significance of women in family literacy programs. Adult students are referred to principally in their roles as "first teachers," "adults," "primary caregivers," and "parents." Gender is evident selectively in women's roles as mothers, which again defines women's learning only in relation to their children. Women tend to be one-dimensional individuals in family literacy theory, research, and program practices.

A gendered perspective on family literacy is important because it urges us to look specifically at women's needs and interests as women, to understand

NEW DIRECTIONS FOR ADULT AND CONTINUING EDUCATION, no. 70, Summer 1996 © Jossey-Bass Publishers

how women have been disenfranchised from the full range of educational opportunities in the first place, and to consider how family literacy programming can either reinforce or challenge gender-related barriers to literacy (Carmack, 1992). In this chapter, we use a gendered perspective to examine the disadvantages for women resulting from the transmission model of literacy that underlies many family literacy programs. (Our transmission model of literacy is adapted from Elsa Auerbach's "transmission of school practices" model in her critique of family literacy programs, 1989; see also Auerbach, 1991.) We suggest how the complexities and conflicts in women's lives, stemming from their multiple roles and responsibilities, needs, and aspirations, can become important factors in family literacy programming. And we end the chapter with specific implications for family literacy practice.

Transmission Model of Family Literacy: A Feminist Critique

Beginning in the mid-1980s, the family and intergenerational literacy movement emerged, in large part, as a creative and economical response to growing poverty and undereducation among women and children. Reports like *A Nation at Risk* (National Commission on Excellence in Education, 1983) suggested more direct educational interventions in families, with parents serving as educational resources for improving children's literacy and schooling. In this *transmission model of literacy,* parents, particularly mothers, are trained to pass on reading skills and other learning behaviors to their children, in an effort "to break the intergenerational cycle of poverty, one family at a time, by changing the 'messages' communicated in the home—messages related to the value of learning to the expectation for success" (National Center for Family Literacy, 1993, p. 1). The assumption is that "the mother's educational background and the family's economic status are the two most significant predictors of a child's success in school" (Darling, 1992, p. 4).

On the surface, the transmission model of literacy learning makes sense; parenting is usually equated with the transfer of knowledge, values, and traditions to children. However, this model is largely prescriptive and does not reflect actual home literacy learning practices documented by recent ethnographic research (Auerbach, 1989; Snow and others, 1991). Further, the model assumes a simplistic cause and effect relationship between women's levels of educational attainment and their children's, with no consideration of such important factors as time spent together or the influence of other family members such as siblings (Auerbach, 1989; Snow and others, 1991). The mother-child relationship is cast as a natural bond rather than as the result of the ways families are organized (Nickse, 1990; Snow and others, 1991; Solsken, 1993; Taylor, 1983) and of the sexual division of labor and power (Laubach Literacy Action, 1993; Luttrell, 1990; Rockhill, 1990; Salice, 1988; Solsken, 1993; Stromquist, 1989). Finally, the model does not specify whether it is reading skills or education that is passed on from generation to generation. How this transmission works to increase social and economic opportunities also remains vaguely specified: for example, "If parents' skills are improved and they learn to value education, their incomes will increase, even as they communicate benefits for education to their children. Families will then be able to support educational efforts of their children more fully" (Brizius, 1993, p. 9).

In addition, the transmission model results in the following specific disadvantages for the women in family literacy programs.

Women as Conduits of Literacy. In the transmission model, women are positioned primarily as carriers of literacy for their families. This "caretaking approach to literacy" (Luttrell, 1990, p. 7) supports women's traditional role in the family and secondary status in society. Slogans such as "teach the mother and reach the child" (Fossen and Sticht, 1991) equate educating women with educating their families. In this view, women pursue literacy education to meet the needs of others and are the first access point in the literacy circuit rather than the subjects of their own learning (Auerbach, 1991; Freire, 1970). They are passive recipients of literacy education rather than active participants. Although called the "first teachers" of their children (Bush, 1989), they are given no authority or power in the teaching role but, instead, are expected to transmit knowledge and skills in prescribed ways. Women's presence in literacy programs becomes esteemed insofar as women convey dominant cultural knowledge and values to their children, knowledge that supports rather than challenges the status quo.

Primary Focus on Children's Learning. A second disadvantage for women, related to the first, is that the transmission model primarily emphasizes educational outcomes for children. Learning activities that maximize benefits to children are stressed; adults receive literacy instruction as a side effect, and their outcomes and "intellectual abilities" have generally been neglected (Fossen and Sticht, 1991, p. 3). The few existing studies have indicated GED attainment as a primary outcome for women students (Seaman, 1992; St. Pierre and others, 1993). Yet there have been virtually no studies of what women learn from reading children's books, helping with homework, or even studying for the GED. The Wider Opportunities for Women (WOW) family literacy program study reported that large percentages of the women already had high school diplomas (49.1 percent) (Fossen and Sticht, 1991).

Greater attention to women's learning and education—and the significance of gender in their learning—may be a means of influencing home literacy practices. Parent advocacy with schools has also been proposed as a better means than the modeling of reading behaviors of enhancing children's school success, with the view that learning such advocacy skills will also increase women's knowledge and their sense of control as they navigate the system (Auerbach, 1989; Rodriguez-Brown and Mulhern, 1993; Gandara, 1989, p. 41).

Devaluation of Women's Home Literacy Practices. As it attempts to introduce school-like literacy learning practices into the home (Auerbach, 1989; Isserlis, 1990), the transmission model may promulgate an educational agenda that is inconsistent with women's standards for mothering, the ways they relate differentially and similarly to their sons and daughters, and the familiar ways they teach and learn with their children. One study (DeTemple and Tabors, 1994) found that mothers read in different ways to their children and bring "their own understandings of how children learn and of what their children need to learn to the book reading situation" (p. 12). Women may resent and resist directive interventions that contradict and devalue their beliefs. For example, one program dropout claimed, "teachers are too involved with trying to change our behavior with children," and another stated, "give us tips on parenting, but don't tell us how to raise our children" (Nurss and Singh, 1993, p. 5). This and other research (Goldsmith, 1995; Rodriguez-Brown and Mulhern, 1993; Zakaluk and Wynes, 1995) indicate the need to build on women's existing practices and the importance of a critical approach that challenges adult students. Little evidence exists that current family literacy programs have a significant impact on women's home literacy practices (Eldridge-Hunter, 1992; St. Pierre and others, 1993) except for more and new reading materials in the home.

Deficiency Images of Mothers. Deficit assumptions about women as mothers abound in transmission models. As Nancy Carmack (1992) and Wendy Luttrell (1990) have discussed, women are considered risks to their children if they lack the skills and values considered necessary for their children's success. It is assumed that women do not communicate the correct educational messages if they are less educated, poor, on welfare, or single or in other ways fail to conform to societal norms for "good mothers." When such assumptions underlie family literacy programs, they may lead women to believe in their own deficiencies as mothers (Luttrell, 1990). In addition, the ultimate goal of many family literacy programs, economic independence for participants (Isserlis, 1990), gives women the additional burden of finding employment and leaving welfare at the same time as they are expected to be spending time and energy at home reading to their children. Such conflicting expectations may lead to women's frustration with the program and eventual dropping out.

Restrictive Modeling of Reading Behavior. The transmission model stresses the importance of the mother in modeling important reading behaviors. Yet this modeling can be an empty experience for the women themselves if the reading is too easy or has little interest or meaning for them or if the language, culture, and gender barriers in the stories are offensive to women or convey negative stereotypes. The meanings derived from reading are too often subordinated to behavioral issues like the correct way to hold a book, question-answering, the amount of reading material in the home, and parents' reading to children (not the reverse). Moreover, reading is often emphasized over writing in family literacy activities, even though writing may be a more empowering experience, as when participants write and read their stories (Auerbach, 1991; Isserlis, 1990). Promoting reading over writing may also reinforce traditional gender norms. Solsken (1993) found that young boys more often prefer the active engagement of writing and girls more often choose the passive (or receptive) activity of reading. Thus, it may be particularly important for girls that women model writing to both their daughters and sons. The typical exclusion of math as a family literacy activity also reinforces gendered norms. Family literacy programs could provide early math preparation for both girls and boys, and one study (Nurss and Singh, 1993) has reported that women were emphatic about receiving more instruction in math and computer skills.

Making Women Visible and Hearing Their Voices

It is time to see women as literacy learners who are at once connected to their children and possessed of their own needs and interests. For women, participation in family literacy programs may be fraught with contradiction and ambivalence, excitement and resistance—feelings that may be related to women's multiple roles in their families and communities. Although many women say, for example, that they come to family literacy programs to be "better mothers" (Luttrell, 1990, p. 14), they may also come as daughters, to fulfill their own parents' dreams for their success, or out of a sense of spiritual commitment, to fulfill a broader life purpose. Viewing women as whole people allows us to design critical and flexible programming that acknowledges and validates women's lives and offers women opportunities to develop diverse skills and challenge restrictive roles.

Realities of Women's Family Lives. Women experience many constraints on their return to school (Horsman, 1990; Rockhill, 1990; Laubach Literacy Action, 1993). Although basic barriers to women's access to education have been addressed through provision of child care, transportation, and flexible scheduling, more complex barriers remain. Women's multiple responsibilities to many different family members (who may include spouses, boyfriends, children and grandchildren, children from the neighborhood and extended family, and aging parents) can produce conflicting demands on their time and resources. Low-income women's lives may be highly mobile and subject to unpredictable changes, particularly if they are highly dependent on others in similarly strained circumstances (Stack, 1974).

Women's views of their family responsibilities and priorities may differ from the program's views of them. Horsman (1990) and others (Carmack, 1992; Laubach Literacy Action, 1993; Rockhill, 1990; Safman, 1986; Seaman, 1992) have discussed the hidden barriers in women's lives, especially women's relationships with violent and abusive men. Such realities can be suppressed if women participants and program staff have few opportunities for open and nonjudgmental communication. When women are encouraged to use the family as an object of critical attention, they may better understand how the constraints they experience have a social rather than an individual base and how gender norms can exacerbate these constraints. They can explore new ways of relating within and among families and receive encouragement for securing more support and increasing control over their lives. The family can shift from a passive precondition for learning into an active subject of learning.

Women's Desire for Change in Their Lives. Many women seek education as a means of moving beyond a restrictive home or work environment and achieving goals of personal growth and independence. One respondent in the Even Start evaluation (St. Pierre and others, 1993) stated that she sought the GED as "the first step toward a better life" (p. 9), and another declared, "[I] wanted to do something with my life" (p. 8). These women echo the women in the Horsman study who sought something "beyond the everyday." Even women who report the desire to read to their children as their main reason for participation typically have more personal goals, ones they may be hesitant to articulate due to social prescriptions against women's pursuit of "selfish" ambitions or due to lack of confidence in their abilities. Answering the needs of women seeking to change, expand, or escape their traditional roles may seem beyond the intent of family literacy programs, but because such programs are one of few educational options accessible to low-income women, it may be critical for them to address these needs, especially if the broader program goal of participant self-sufficiency and autonomy is taken seriously. To succeed, women need more than a GED, more than functional literacy and parenting skills. They need activities that allow them to explore career options, develop advocacy and critical thinking skills (Auerbach, 1989; Carmack, 1992; Rodriguez-Brown and Mulhern, 1993), and envision new futures for themselves as well as their children.

Women's Conflicts in Gaining New Skills. Rockhill's study (1990) offers evocative evidence of the ambivalence associated with women's pursuit of literacy. She describes literacy as both "desire" and "threat" for women; desired for the independence it offers but threatening in its potential impact on women's family relationships and their nurturing role as mothers. Women come to feel differently about their family roles as they gain new skills and confidence (Isserlis, 1990), particularly if they traditionally subordinated their own needs to those of their families (Rockhill, 1990). Their responsibilities for children may emerge as major barriers to their own learning and self-discovery. One study found that some parents wanted less rather than more program time with their children (Nurss and Singh, 1993), and women may feel that children's "noises" of literacy in the classroom interfere with their own learning (Isserlis, 1990). Husbands, when included in programming, may resist women's educational efforts when they threaten power relationships within the home (Rockhill, 1990). Family literacy educators who recognize that the family may be an obstacle rather than an aid to transformation can help women understand and resolve the tensions between their home and school lives.

Cultural Differences Among Women. Women's roles, expectations, and experiences with their children differ because they are products of histories and contexts arising from different racial, religious, and cultural identities. Ethnographic research such as that of Heath (1982), for example, has documented class-related differences among communities in parent and child literacy learning practices. Differences of race, culture, and class may contribute to differences in women's goals and suggest the kinds of classroom-initiated literacy practices they will find compatible. Research (Purcell-Gates, L'Allier, and Smith, 1995) suggests that broad generalizations about race, class, or cultural differences disguise the complexity and diversity of individual behavior and family life. Understanding and respecting individuals' differences are integral to family literacy programming that neither fosters stereotypes nor imposes a singular cultural model, denying participants their own values and traditions.

What Is to Be Done? Implications for Family Literacy Practice

Literacy programs can take a number of practical steps to increase their value and utility to women.

Critical Reflection and Leadership Development. The Laubach Literacy Action report on women's literacy education (1993) made numerous recommendations for addressing obvious and hidden educational barriers. Two suggestions particularly relevant here are increased emphasis on critical reflection and increased emphasis on leadership development for women. Women can be encouraged to critically reflect on the traditional role of women in the family, how this role is freeing or oppressive, and alternative models of family relations. A curriculum that validates different family structures and values yet reveals that individuals can rethink their roles in new and liberating ways is important.

Teaching women to critically read children's storybooks is another way to stimulate reflection and make reading a "transformational" activity (Goldsmith, 1995). Parents can be encouraged to read against the story line, question an author's assumptions, and relate ideas to their own lives and experiences. Goldsmith (1995) describes the use of children's stories to explore social issues and values, proposing that "family literacy programs can provide the occasion for adults to deepen their conversations. From these conversations will emerge . . . a stronger sense of who we are and perhaps a greater willingness to let go of some of what doesn't serve us" (p. 562).

Developing women's leadership is important if women are to move into decision-making roles in their communities. Participatory education approaches (Auerbach, 1991; Fingeret and Jurmo, 1989) allow women to assume leadership roles in the classroom and in program management. Edwards (1995), for example, describes how four low-income mothers successfully took leadership for a parent-child book-reading program. Such experiences are stepping stones to broader leadership activities. Women leaders from the community can be recruited as speakers, role models, and mentors for women developing leadership skills.

Challenging Gender Stereotypes. Teaching women to identify and actively resist gender stereotypes is essential. For example, women can be asked to identify stereotypes and biases in classroom texts, popular fiction, television programs, films, and other media. Discussion of stereotypes' impact on their own and others' self-perceptions can reveal and challenge limiting assumptions about women's and men's roles and abilities. Teaching mothers to identify sexist and racist biases can help them select appropriate books for their children. They can learn to question gender stereotypes while reading with children, calling attention to the portrayal of girls as helpless or passive while boys are active and adventurous. Mothers and their children might envision alternatives by creating "feminist fairy tales" (Gilbert and Taylor, 1991), reconstructing old story lines to challenge or reverse gendered norms.

Teaching women how to confront the gender biases they encounter can also become part of family literacy instruction. Sexual harassment and more covert forms of gender discrimination can be topics for reading, discussion, and skill development. Mothers can also help their children resist gender biases encountered in school. For example, parents and children can learn to confront counselors or teachers who discourage girls from pursuing scientific or technical occupations. They can learn advocacy skills to petition schools for prenatal care and parenting classes that include fathers as well as mothers.

Involving Men from the Community. Encouraging greater numbers of men to participate in family literacy programs supports women and ensures that children see men involved in an activity that many might otherwise consider "women's work." Male teachers, ministers, community service workers, retirees, and grandparents can be recruited from the community if male family members are unavailable or resistant, and such broader involvement can communicate the idea that education is a responsibility of communities, not only individuals and families. Holland (1991) describes the recruitment of male volunteers as role models in inner-city elementary schools, an example of how men might be trained and supported in taking a more active, positive part in young children's learning experiences.

Recruiting male teachers to literacy programs is also critical. Obtaining nonsexist and interesting reading material for men as well as women is important to promote gender-sensitive programming and a supportive environment in which men can receive literacy instruction. Finally, women's and men's discussing together why men do not play a greater part in the education of children may relocate men as important figures in this endeavor, shifting educational responsibility away from women alone.

School as a Family for Literacy Learning. In the Even Start evaluation (St. Pierre and others, 1993), one student commented that the school had become a family for her. A participant in another study described teachers as "big sisters" (Nurss and Singh, 1993, p. 8). Fostering such intimacy and support among literacy program participants and staff can be central to learning. According to the FLAME report, building community was important to enabling the participants to "take risks, learn from other parents and make friends" (Shanahan, Mulhern, and Rodriguez-Brown, 1995, p. 590). In Sissel's study (1995) of two Head Start programs, she found that a sense of being part of a family sustained women's involvement. Regarding the child's classroom as a family and involving parents have been suggested by others (Cairney, 1995; Handel, 1995), but viewing the adult education setting as a family is new. It reflects the concept of *connected education* (Belenky, Clinchy, Goldberger, and Tarule, 1986; Carmack, 1992), in which women are encouraged to support each other's growth in group learning situations and to hear each other's stories. Teachers should not necessarily be viewed as parents, but they need to provide positive models of caring, understanding, assertiveness, and mutual learning. In such an environment, family members might be encouraged to assist each other in resolving and negotiating problems and to practice new workable ways of relating.

Ask Women About Literacy Goals, Beliefs, and Experiences. Encouraging women to share their literacy goals, beliefs, and experiences enables them to develop a personal voice and validates them as people, learners, and teachers in their families and communities. Offering women the opportunity to create their own stories, share them with children, and publish them may be more empowering than reading commercial texts. The Book Bridges (Zakaluk and Wynes, 1995) and Literacy Volunteers of America–Chippewa Valley (Goethel, 1995) programs offer good examples of fostering all aspects of writing development and emphasize writing based on students' personal experiences. Book Bridges participants move from writing biographies of each other to writing biographies of family members and family stories. Such activities can increase insight into family dynamics, celebrate family strengths, and challenge restrictive family roles.

Listening to women's voices and needs on the community level is also important in program development. Project WILL (Women in Laubach Literacy) (McIvor, 1990) is a model program for recruiting and retaining women participants. Through a community analysis, program planners learned that over half of the county's low-literate population were women but that women were a very small proportion of adult education participants. The program reduced barriers by providing support such as transportation; it integrated significant women's issues in the curriculum; it is open to women who are not mothers (communicating that women's education need not be tied to the parental role), and it is located on a university campus, emphasizing the women's student status with an environment that is academic and encourages continued education. The programmers report that "during breaks, the women sit on benches outside and absorb the [university] atmosphere around them. Like university students, the women leave the campus carrying books" (p. 32).

Push for Women's Continued Education. Family literacy programs should not be considered the last educational stop for low-literate women if they are to obtain meaningful employment and long-term financial self-sufficiency. The current lack of attention to higher education for low-income women is surprising considering that some studies have suggested a link between continuing education, higher incomes, and literacy levels for women (Barton and Jenkins, 1995). A 1987 evaluation study (Rice, 1993) found that in sixty-one Work Incentive (WIN) demonstration programs, only a little over 1 percent of the AFDC recipients continued with their education and that few programs promoted college education. The problem is that "higher education as a route out of poverty or more generally, as a policy option and right of poor women, has yet to be legitimized philosophically or strategically" (Rice, 1993, p. 11).

Furthering adult education is a legitimate component of family literacy programming (Literacy Volunteers of America, 1991; Sticht, 1995). Gaining support for it will be challenging but not impossible. Women can become political advocates for their education by joining with other women to write to policy makers and to organize to demand welfare policies that support women's higher education. Teachers can counsel women about a variety of educational and career opportunities and encourage them to visit colleges and vocational schools, promoting the idea that women's further education is as important as their children's.

Conclusion

When family literacy programming allows women to explore a full range of options in their lives, when mothers and daughters, grandparents, and community members can learn and teach each other in an open, safe, and intellectually stimulating environment, when fathers and other male community members are involved in children's education, and when women have a full range of educational opportunities, then family literacy programs will have achieved a major goal in overcoming gender biases. Perhaps more than any other type of programming, family literacy has the opportunity to challenge the cycle of gender and educational subordination for low-income women and to facilitate positive and progressive changes, meeting rather than defeating women's dreams for their futures.

References

Auerbach, E. "Toward a Social-Contextual Approach to Family Literacy." *Harvard Educational Review,* 1989, 59 (2), 165–181.

Auerbach, E. "Rosa's Challenge: Connecting Classrooms and Community Contexts." In S. Benesch (ed.), *ESL in America: Myths and Possibilities.* Portsmouth, N.H.: Heinemann, 1991.

Barton, P., and Jenkins, L. *Literacy and Dependency.* Princeton, N.J.: Educational Testing Service, 1995.

Belenky, M. F., Clinchy, B. M., Goldberger, N. R., and Tarule, J. M. *Women's Ways of Knowing: The Development of Self, Voice, and Mind.* New York: Basic Books, 1986.

Brizius, J. A. *Generation to Generation: Realizing the Promise of Family Literacy.* National Center for Family Literacy. Ypsilanti, Mich.: High/Scope Press, 1993.

Bush, B. *First Teachers.* Washington, D.C.: Barbara Bush Foundation for Family Literacy, 1989.

Cairney, T. H. "Developing Parent Partnerships in Secondary Literacy Learning." *Journal of Reading,* 1995, 38 (7), 520–521.

Carmack, N. A. "Women and Illiteracy: The Need for Gender-Specific Programming in Literacy Education." *Adult Basic Education,* 1992, 2 (3), 176–194.

Darling, S. *Family Literacy: The Need and the Promise.* Louisville, Ky.: National Center for Family Literacy, 1992.

DeTemple, J. M., and Tabors, P. O. "Styles of Interaction During Book Reading Tasks: Implications for Literacy Intervention with Low-Income Families." Paper presented at the 44th National Reading Conference, San Diego, 1994.

Edwards, P. A. "Empowering Low-Income Mothers and Fathers to Share Books with Young Children." *Reading Teacher,* 1995, *48* (7), 558–564.

Eldridge-Hunter, D. "Intergenerational Literacy: Impact on the Development of the Storybook Reading Behaviors of Hispanic Mothers." In C. Kinzer (ed.), *Literacy, Research, Theory and Practice: Views from Many Perspectives.* Chicago: National Reading Conference, 1992.

Fingeret, A., and Jurmo, P. (eds.). *Participatory Literacy Education.* New Directions for Continuing Education, no. 42. San Francisco: Jossey-Bass, 1989.

Fossen, S. V., and Sticht, T. G. *Teach the Mother and Reach the Child: Results of the Intergenerational Literacy Action Research Project of Wider Opportunities for Women.* Washington, D.C.: Wider Opportunities for Women, 1991.

Freire, P. *Pedagogy of the Oppressed.* New York: Seabury Press, 1970.

Gandara, P. "Those Children Are Ours: Moving Toward Community." *NEA Today,* 1989, 7 (6), 38–43.

Gilbert, P., and Taylor, S. *Fashioning the Feminine: Girls, Popular Culture, and Schooling.* North Sydney, Australia: Allen & Unwin, 1991.

Goethel, J. "Writing: The Golden Thread in Family Learning." *Adult Learning,* 1995, 7 (2), 26–27.

Goldsmith, E. "Deepening the Conversation." *Journal of Reading,* 1995, *38* (7), 558–563.

Handel, R. D. "Family Reading at the Middle School." *Journal of Reading,* 1995, *38* (7), 528–539.

Heath, S. B. *Ways with Words: Language, Life and Work in Communities and Classrooms.* New York: Cambridge University Press, 1982.

Holland, S. "Positive Role Models for Primary-Grade Black Inner-City Males." *Equity & Excellence,* 1991, *25* (1), 40–44.

Horsman, J. *Something in My Mind Besides the Everyday: Women and Literacy.* Toronto: WomenUs Press, 1990.

Isserlis, J. "On Women, Literacy and Learning: An Investigation." Unpublished paper, 1990. (ED 324 985)

Laubach Literacy Action. *By Women/For Women: A Beginning Dialogue on Women and Literacy in the United States.* Syracuse, N.Y.: Laubach Literacy International, 1993.

Literacy Volunteers of America. *How to Add Family Literacy to Your Program.* Syracuse, N.Y.: Literacy Volunteers of America, 1991.

Luttrell, W. "Taking Care of Literacy: A Feminist Critique." Unpublished paper, Department of Sociology, Duke University, 1990.

McIvor, C. (ed.). *Family Literacy in Action: A Survey of Successful Programs.* Syracuse, N.Y.: New Readers Press, 1990.

National Center for Family Literacy. *NCFL Newsletter,* 1993, *5* (3).

National Commission on Excellence in Education. *A Nation at Risk: The Imperative for Educational Reform.* Washington, D.C.: U.S. Department of Education, 1983.

Nickse, R. S. *Family and Intergenerational Literacy Programs: An Update of "The Noises of Literacy."* ERIC Information Series, no. 342. Columbus: Center on Education and Training for Employment, Ohio State University, 1990.

Nurss, J., and Singh, R. *Atlanta Family Literacy Collaborative: Interviews of Participants: Years 1 and 2.* Atlanta: Atlanta Family Literacy Collaborative, 1993.

Purcell-Gates, V., L'Allier, S., and Smith, D. "Literacy at the Harts' and the Larsons': Diversity Among Poor, Inner-City Families." *Reading Teacher,* 1995, *48* (7), 572–578.

Rice, J. K. "Back to School: Women, Welfare and Access to Higher Education." *Adult Learning,* May/June 1993, pp. 10–11, 23.

Rockhill, K. "Literacy as Threat/Desire: Longing to be SOMEBODY." *TESL-Talk,* 1990, *20* (1), 89–110.

Rodriguez-Brown, F. V., and Mulhern, M. "Fostering Critical Literacy Through Family Literacy: A Study of Families in a Mexican-Immigrant Community." *Bilingual Research Journal*, 1993, *17* (3–4), 1–17.

Safman, P. *Illiterate Women: New Approaches for New Lives*. Paper presented at the American Association for Adult and Continuing Education conference, Hollywood, Fla., Oct. 1986.

St. Pierre, R., Swartz, J., Murray, S., Deck, D., and Nickel, P. *National Evaluation of the Even Start Family Literacy Program*. Report on Effectiveness. Cambridge, Mass.: ABT Associates, 1993.

Salice, B. *Women and Illiteracy in the United States: A Feminist View: Revised*. Unpublished manuscript, 1988. (ED 299 434)

Seaman, D. F. "Follow-Up Study of the Impact of the Kenan Trust Model." *Adult Basic Education*, 1992, *2* (2), 71–83.

Shanahan, T., Mulhern, M., and Rodriguez-Brown, F. "Project FLAME: Lessons Learned from a Family Literacy Program for Linguistic Minorities." *Reading Teacher*, 1995, *48* (7), 586–593.

Sissel, P. A. "Capacity, Power, and Connection: An Ethnographic Study of Parents, Learning, and Project Head Start." Unpublished doctoral dissertation, Graduate School of Education, Rutgers, the State University of New Jersey, 1995.

Snow, C. E., Barnes, W. S., Chandler, J., Goodman, I. F., and Hemphill, L. *Unfulfilled Expectations: Home and School Influences on Literacy*. Cambridge, Mass.: Harvard University Press, 1991.

Solsken, J. *Literacy, Gender and Work*. Norwood, N.J.: Ablex, 1993.

Stack, C. B. *All Our Kin: Strategies for Survival in a Black Community*. New York: HarperCollins, 1974.

Sticht, T. G. "Adult Education for Family Literacy." *Adult Learning*, Nov./Dec. 1995, pp. 23–24.

Stromquist, N. P. "Challenges to the Attainment of Women's Literacy." Revised paper presented at the symposium "Women and Literacy: Yesterday, Today, and Tomorrow," sponsored by the Nordic Association for the Study of Education in Developing Countries, Hasselby, Sweden, June 1989.

Taylor, D. *Family Literacy: Young Children Learning to Read and Write*. Portsmouth, N.H.: Heinemann, 1983.

Zakaluk, B. L., and Wynes, B. J. "Book Bridges: A Family Literacy Program for Immigrant Women." *Journal of Reading*, 1995, *38* (7), 550–557.

SONDRA CUBAN is a doctoral student in the School of Library and Information Studies, University of Wisconsin–Madison.

ELISABETH HAYES is associate professor of continuing and vocational education at the University of Wisconsin–Madison.

The African American community's struggle for literacy occurs in the context of liberation.

Our Students, Ourselves: Lessons of Challenge and Hope from the African American Community

Elizabeth A. Peterson

At the end of this century, low literacy proficiency among adult African Americans is a problem of tremendous proportion. Without the skills to acquire a meaningful job, many of those who have been left out or have dropped out end up in the growing permanent underclass. This phenomenon is especially disturbing because historically for African Americans, the struggle from slavery to freedom has been seen as a struggle for education (defined primarily as literacy) and for educational opportunity that would lead to economic equality and freedom. This chapter focuses on the historical, social, and economic factors that have exacerbated the problem of black illiteracy in the United States and explores the ramifications of race and ethnicity for future literacy programs.

The Crisis: Changing Realities

Depending on how one defines the target population, there are between 50 million and 70 million adults in the United States who have limited literacy levels, and the relationship between such limited literacy and social and economic status is clear. According to Beder (1991), "Low-literates tend to be less affluent, to be more frequently unemployed and underemployed, and have attained less schooling" (p. 30). The children of these individuals are more likely to be disadvantaged and to grow up in poverty. They are the ones we now label "at risk."

One factor contributing to the increased numbers of low-literate adults is the growing sophistication of the population as a whole. In 1930, the Census

NEW DIRECTIONS FOR ADULT AND CONTINUING EDUCATION, no. 70, Summer 1996 © Jossey-Bass Publishers 17

Bureau defined the illiterate person as one who "cannot write in any language" (Gray, 1939, p. 19). In today's technological society, individuals must learn skills that go far beyond this simple definition if they are to continually advance themselves and acquire the training and retraining demanded by new information and technology. Thus, the National Literacy Act of 1991 redefined literacy as one's "ability to read, write, and speak in English, and to compute and solve problems at levels of proficiency necessary to function on the job and in society, to achieve one's goals, and develop one's knowledge and potential" (Public Law 102–73, Section 3, 1991).

Technological and societal changes have increased African Americans' educational disadvantage. However, it is important for us to be aware that the basic fact of educational disadvantage goes back to the days of slavery. Indeed, the educational needs of African Americans were largely overlooked up until the 1960s. Before that time, the undereducation of African Americans was a legally employed means of conscious control that whites exercised in order to subjugate slaves and laborers. Although the civil rights movement brought an end to legal discrimination, racist attitudes continue to influence educational practice. Colin and Preciphs (1991) define racism as "conscious or unconscious, and expressed in actions or attitudes initiated by individuals, groups, or institutions that treat human beings unjustly because of their skin pigmentation" (p. 62). Racism is at work when issues and concerns that seem to affect primarily African Americans receive little or no attention from people who could make a difference. Ogbu (1983) supports this position and contends that "the clear connection between educational achievement and adult economic participation serves to encourage whites to persevere and achieve in school. African Americans, however, have been faced with a reality where educational attainment does not necessarily bring the benefits that it brings to whites. This serves to discourage them from committing to, and persisting in, the schooling process" (p. 139).

Although individuals from all ethnic and racial groups in this society suffer from undereducation, for many, illiteracy wears a black face. In the 1930s, the adult education director for the state of South Carolina advocated increased support for adult education even though many felt that illiteracy was simply a "Negro problem" (Gray, 1939). She recognized the potential severity of the problem and foresaw many of the social problems that we face today: "In the final analysis [illiteracy] means impoverished homes, excessive birth and death rates, low cultural standards, and prejudiced outlooks. It nurtures and spreads disease; it fosters race prejudice and class hatred; it lowers standards of wages; it lessens production and restricts consumption; it prevents intelligent participation in civic affairs which is dependent on judgment drawn from the printed page; it is inconsistent with a democratic society" (Gray, 1939, p. 20).

According to the National Adult Literacy Survey (Kirsch, Jungeblut, Jenkins, and Kolstad, 1993) approximately 44 percent of African Americans and 54 percent of Hispanic Americans may be classified as functionally illiterate.

Robert Eng (1987) writes that "the problem of black literacy is part of a continuum of problems afflicting black America" (p. 16). Black undereducation and racial prejudice have become inextricably intertwined, and racism may be the one factor that will keep the disparity between the rich and poor intact. In the 1990s, we are, with the erosion of the middle class, becoming a two-class society. Even though there are more black professionals with advanced degrees than ever before, the majority of African Americans are making up an underclass. Moreover, although the causal relationship between illiteracy, poverty, and criminal behavior is difficult to determine, it is believed that there is a connection. Ogbu, for example, believes that the lack of equitable economic rewards for African Americans is not a consequence but a root cause of school failure and low literacy (Fitzsimmons, 1991). Less educated persons are less likely to have the resources and skills required to obtain and keep gainful employment. Out of ignorance or desperation, they may resort to drastic means to support themselves or their families, with incarceration as the result.

Eng (1987) believes that the problem of illiteracy and its consequences has now advanced "beyond the ability and responsibility of blacks to solve it alone" (p. 16). And he cautions against the return to isolation pushed by some black leaders. Although integration as it presently exists has done little to improve the quality of education for African Americans, Eng believes it is ill conceived to romanticize segregation. The goal remains integration, which was never achieved, not simply desegregation. "The goal . . . was equal access to opportunity without regard to color or race" (p. 16), because given equal access, Eng asserts, blacks achieve equally. He charges that rather than allow blacks equal access, white Americans have chosen to devalue and demean public education as a whole, especially in areas in which blacks are the primary beneficiaries.

Regardless of one's perspective on the causes, the reality is that public education is failing black children in large numbers. Yet African Americans who fall out or drop out of the public school system often return through adult education and literacy programs, hoping for a second chance. One study of illiteracy among the homeless revealed that although whites continued to be the largest group served by homeless programs, African Americans made up a large proportion of learners in nine states: California, 36 percent; New York, 60 percent; Missouri, 51 percent; Massachusetts, 35 percent; Delaware, 73 percent; North Carolina, 57 percent; Michigan, 65 percent; Mississippi, 51 percent; and Ohio, 53 percent (Office of Vocational Education and Adult Education, 1993). Yet once enrolled, they find themselves in a program considered by many professional educators to be only a stepchild of the educational system.

The Promise: Toward a More Just Nation

At the beginning of the twentieth century, despite the insidious racism practiced in the United States, African Americans were hoping to achieve equality through self-improvement and educational uplift. Indeed, African Americans, like most citizens, have long conceived of education as a basic right and desired it for their children. They have maintained "an unstinting belief in the power of literacy to effect essential political, cultural, social, and economic change" (Harris, 1992, p. 276). Booker T. Washington, Mary McCleod Bethune, W.E.B. DuBois, and countless other black leaders and educators continually stressed the importance of education for the uplift of the African American people and dedicated their lives to educating their people. However, they may have underestimated the strength of racism's clutch on U.S. society. Harris contends that education was never bestowed upon African Americans by an enlightened citizenry. Rather, African Americans "demanded, created, funded, and maintained educational institutions that would provide literacy for all, apprise individuals of and prepare them for the dominating culture's institutions, counteract the pernicious and venal images of African Americans prevalent in the popular culture, and engender group solidarity and commitment to uplift" (p. 276). Tracing African American conceptions of literacy in broad historical periods, Harris's work constitutes a framework for considering the events, individuals, ideologies, and institutions that have shaped current African American beliefs and attitudes toward literacy and schooling.

It was during the period from 1700 to 1799 that the "seeds of literacy" were planted, although not without hardship or opposition: most of the then slave states prohibited teaching slaves to read, and African Americans learned by themselves, often defying their "masters" and struggling independently or in small groups after long hours of work. Literate blacks were often extremely aware of the deeper meaning of their actions (Foster, 1993). Phillis Wheatley, for example, often forced by her owners to read before their guests and to write spontaneous verse on topics she was provided, kept diaries that showed she knew she was also defying the stereotype. She was living proof that people of African descent were intelligent beings. In the North, where no codified restrictions on black education existed, religious denominations including the Quakers, some Puritans, and the Anglicans started schools for black students. The primary impetus for literacy was African Americans' concern that literacy was needed in order to acquire freedom and power. African American leaders pushed for the establishment of benevolent organizations, societies, schools, and libraries to serve African American children. Richard Allen, founder of the African Methodist Episcopal Church in 1794, was very vocal in advocating for African American liberty, education, and economic independence (Harris, 1992, p. 278).

During the next period delineated by Harris, 1800 to 1859, the number of African Americans who could read rose to approximately 15 to 20 percent. Belief in education, particularly higher education, as a means of advancing African Americans flourished, and debate among African Americans over the type of education that would be most beneficial (basic, vocational, or classical) began. Schools were founded for those who sought to continue their education; Avery College and Lincoln University are two historically black schools that were founded at this time. Several mainstream postsecondary institutions began to accept black students.

African American participation in all forms of education increased significantly during the period from 1860 to 1899. Approximately 20 percent of African Americans were literate by this time. Immediately following the Civil War, newly freed African Americans "rushed to create and attend makeshift schools in droves" (Harris, 1992, p. 280), struggling to acquire the education and skills that would enable them to prosper as free men and women. Harris argues that the most significant testament to the African American desire for literacy during this time was the push for the establishment of free public schools for all children. Also for the first time, gender discrimination was recognized as being as pervasive as racial discrimination.

The period between 1900 and 1939 represents a "golden age" in African American education (Harris, 1992, p. 281). Different and sometimes opposing ideologies flourished during this period, symbolized by the three educational scholars, Booker T. Washington, W.E.B. DuBois, and Carter G. Woodson. Washington, in his now infamous "Atlanta Compromise," proposed that African Americans postpone the press for racial equality to place more emphasis on education in the practical skills needed by farmers, tradesmen, and laborers. Critics charged that the premise that a skilled, hardworking black population would overcome racism was false and that Washington's position legitimized white efforts to subjugate freedmen. DuBois, one of Washington's most vocal critics, felt that equality was always the first and foremost goal and that African Americans should obtain the highest academic degrees possible. The black masses would achieve equality through the leadership of a group of talented individuals (the "talented tenth" of the black population) armed with a classical education of the finest caliber. Woodson's views were similar. Arguing that the "Negro" had been "miseducated" to believe that blacks benefited from the education that whites provided for them, he challenged blacks to reconsider the logic of believing that those who had enslaved and oppressed blacks would reverse themselves and become benefactors. According to Woodson ([1933] 1990), self-help was the answer: "The Negro needs to become angry with himself because he has not handled his own affairs wisely. In other words, the Negro must learn from others how to take care of himself in this trying ordeal. He must not remain content with taking over what others set aside for him and then come in the guise of friends to subject even that limited information to further misinterpretation" (p. 197).

By 1930, the celebration of African American culture known as the Harlem Renaissance had increased wealthy philanthropists' interest in African American education. The Carnegie Corporation funded the Negro Experiments in adult education under the auspices of the American Association of Adult Education. Harlem and Atlanta experiments were "planned as attempts to discern the kind of adult education most appropriate for African Americans" (Guy, 1996, p. 92). Another leader who made a tremendous contribution to African American literacy during the "golden age" was Marcus Garvey. Garvey sought to overturn the "effectiveness of white control and oppressive constraints" that resulted in African American dependency. Through the creation of the Universal Negro Improvement Association and the African Communities League (UNIA-ACL), he implemented educational programs that promoted positive self-ethnic images. Garvey's "clearly defined educational goals" were a precursor to present-day Afrocentric approaches to education: "First, the eradication of the influence of fatalism. . . . Second, the development of selfethnic consciousness, selfethnic identity, selfethnic reliance, selfethnic unity, development of a racial code (the Philosophy of African Fundamentalism), development of good character, and selfethnic knowledge through historical study. Third, leadership development: social, cultural, economic and political" (Colin, 1996, p. 55).

The last period outlined by Harris (1940 to 1992) is marked by African Americans' effort to become influential participants in U.S. society. Several major events in this period changed the course of this nation and also changed the structure, focus, and delivery of adult literacy programs. They were the 1954 decision in *Brown v. Topeka Board of Education,* the civil rights movement, the War on Poverty begun in 1964, and the passage of the Adult Education Act of 1966. *Brown v. Topeka Board of Education,* which made school segregation unconstitutional, marked the beginning of what would be known as the civil rights movement. (It was also in the aftermath of the *Brown* decision that a young minister named Martin Luther King, Jr., rose to prominence.) The civil rights movement clearly linked basic education and the right to participate as a citizen in the United States. Initially, the unifying cause in the movement was not to learn how to read and write but to gain access to the political system by using the power of the vote. Acquiring literacy skills was a hoped-for means to that end and to a society that allowed more of its citizens a voice, access to the political system, and an opportunity to compete equally for jobs, which in turn would improve the quality of life. The chains of oppression that had existed since slavery would finally be broken.

In the 1970s and later, although many African Americans continued to believe in integration, "a reassessment began that emphasized the need to encourage philosophies and curricula that affirmed the value of African Americans and their culture and that enabled them to acquire the literacy needed to function in an advanced technological society. Indeed, the need for independent schools became apparent, especially those that were nationalist or Pan Africanist" (Harris, 1992, p. 283). Recently, African American educators have proposed Afrocentric educational practices based on traditional black values (Asante, 1989; Kunjufu, 1985, 1986; Madhubuti, 1989). The seven basic values of African society are *Umoia* (unity), *Kujichaqulia* (self-determination), *Ujima* (collective work and responsibility), *Ujamaa* (cooperative economics), *Nia* (purpose), *Kuumb* (creativity), and *Imani* (faith). An approach that emphasizes these values may "ensure that students complete schooling literate and in possession of positive self images" (Harris, 1992, p. 284).

The Challenge: Continuing the Struggle for Equality

The African American community faces several tremendous obstacles as it continues the struggle for social, economic, and political power into the 1990s. Many African American educators, students, and activists continue to believe that education is still the primary weapon against poverty and oppression (Gadsden, 1992), and many African Americans who return to Adult Basic Education (ABE) and other literacy programs do so because they continue to believe that education is the great equalizer. Critics in the black community are challenging this long-held assumption, however. The role of class and sociopolitical contexts in education is being challenged, particularly by black youths, who are critical of the structure and configuration of existing knowledge delivery systems. Even the value of literacy itself is being questioned. In one study, black teenagers known to be above average were found to be refusing to excel in school because to do so meant to "be white" (Moniz and Bolton, 1991, p. 1A). For these young people, the educational system was further evidence of manipulation by white society.

Once again, there are cries for more community involvement and control over education. There are demands for a more Afrocentric curriculum and instructors with sensitivity to African American culture and experiences. Quigley found that students enrolled in ABE programs often dropped out of school initially due to insensitive teachers, peer group pressure, irrelevant subject matter, boredom, racism, and problems with school rules. As adults, they resisted continuing their education for personal and emotive reasons (child care, transportation, and scheduling problems); cultural and ideological reasons (presumed racism, peer pressure, and boredom); and age-related concerns (feelings of being "too old to learn"). Although they thought education had a potential social and economic value for their children and for others, they did not find it of value for themselves; having experienced failure in the past, they saw little reason to pursue schooling now.

In another study (Peterson, 1996), African American adult education program directors in South Carolina described racism as the major challenge they faced. For example, one such director explained that "after desegregation there was much discussion about what to do with all the black administrators that were displaced after the closing of the black schools. Previously, almost every school district had two superintendents, one white and one black. The solution: the white superintendent maintained his position and the black superintendent became the adult education director" (personal communication to author). The adult education program directors also thought they were always fighting an uphill battle, that illiteracy is still viewed as primarily a black problem and that money is allotted with that in mind. They did not feel it was an accident that regions with large black populations are also among the poorest regions and lack the resources needed to educate and train black youths and adults for a changing job market. They felt they had been victims of discrimination, that white educational policy makers were insensitive to the needs of poor and uneducated black people, and that much of the progress they had made in their own communities was due to their own aggressiveness. Subtle racism was always at work to keep poor blacks "in their place."

The Dream: The Chain Is Broken

It is reasonable to say that African Americans who are most in need of literacy services face many personal and situational barriers. Lack of dependable child care, transportation, support, and financial resources presents real challenges to those who wish to return to school to improve their skills. If the ultimate goal is to break the bonds of illiteracy, more support in addressing these challenges needs to be given to adult students and the programs that serve them. In addition, many potential adult students have deep emotional reasons for resisting basic skills and literacy programs. "Previous experiences in school combined with skepticism that ABE would be anything other than another type of school plays a major part" (Quigley, 1995, p. 6). Special care needs to be taken to ensure that the program environment does not repeat the school environment and its negative experiences.

The history of African American educational experience and thought described here suggests these specific implications for literacy programs:

Teachers and tutors should be trained to be sensitive to cultural matters; specific instruction on the use of the seven traditional black values is essential.
Literacy programs should use a curriculum that focuses on basic skills and simultaneously promotes a positive African American self-ethnic image.
Course design should include an "unlearning" component, to overcome previous negative associations with schooling.
Leadership should stress the need for and support of legislation that funds literacy programs for adults. Seen as a stepchild or even, in the words of an adult education director, a "dumping ground" of the educational system (personal communication to author), adult education programs have received fewer funds and other resources than they need to achieve their goals.
More African American community members should be involved in adult education, especially as instructors, facilitators, and mentors.

Historically, African Americans have viewed literacy as the means of the eventual liberation of the entire race. However, it is now clear that only with considerable care, foresight, and leadership will the chains of illiteracy be broken. Compounding the outlook for the future is the current reality that adult education programs, along with many other social programs, are at risk of losing funding. Yet the struggle continues and in spite of many obstacles, real progress has been made. We must continue to pass on the legacy of literacy to future generations, and "as we teach the descendants of some true believers in education," we must "enable them to expand the meanings of literacy—to build on, or embellish, the legacy of literacy for personal and community development for generations to come" (Gadsden, 1992, p. 335).

Conclusion: A Seed of Hope

Illiteracy has already cost this nation billions of dollars in lost income and taxes and in money spent on welfare programs and prisons. The loss of human potential is nowhere more greatly seen than in the African American community. But this is a problem that can be solved. As in the past, African Americans must recognize the connection between education and freedom and involve themselves in the effort to make a variety of literacy services available and accessible to all who are in need.

References

Asante, M. *Afrocentricity.* Trenton, N.J.: Africa World Press, 1989.

Beder, H. *Adult Literacy: Issues for Policy and Practice.* Malabar, Fla.: Krieger, 1991.

Colin, S.A.J., III. "Marcus Garvey: Africentric Adult Education for Selfethnic Reliance." In E. Peterson (ed.), *Freedom Road: Adult Education of African Americans.* Malabar, Fla.: Krieger, 1996.

Colin, S.A.J., III, and Preciphs, T. "Perceptual Patterns and the Learning Environments: Confronting White Racism." In R. Hiemstra (ed.), *Creating Environments for Effective Adult Learning.* New Directions for Adult and Continuing Education, no. 50. San Francisco: Jossey-Bass, 1991.

Eng, R. "Historical Perspectives on the Problem of Black Illiteracy." *Educational Horizons,* 1987, *66* (1), 13–17.

Fitzsimmons, K. "African American Women Who Persist in Literacy Programs: An Exploratory Study." *Urban Review,* 1991, *23* (4), 231–250.

Foster, F. S. *Written by Herself: Literary Production by African American Women.* Bloomington: Indiana University Press, 1993.

Gadsden, V. L. "Giving Meaning to Literacy: Intergenerational Beliefs About Access." *Theory into Practice,* 1992, *31* (4), 328–336.

Gray, W. L. *The 21st Annual Report of the State Supervisor of Adult Schools.* Columbia: South Carolina State Department of Education, 1939.

Guy, T. C. "The American Association of Adult Education and the Experiments in African American Adult Education." In E. Peterson (ed.), *Freedom Road: Adult Education of African Americans.* Malabar, Fla.: Krieger, 1996.

Harris, V. J. "African-American Conceptions of Literacy: A Historical Perspective." *Theory into Practice,* 1992, *31* (4), 276–296.

Kirsch, I. S., Jungeblut, A., Jenkins, L., and Kolstad, A. *Adult Literacy in America: A First Look at the Results of the National Adult Literacy Survey (NALS).* Washington, D.C.: National Center for Educational Statistics, U.S. Department of Education, 1993.

Kunjufu, J. *The Conspiracy to Destroy Black Boys.* Vol. 1. Chicago: Afro-Am, 1985.

Kunjufu, J. *The Conspiracy to Destroy Black Boys.* Vol. 2. Chicago: Afro-Am, 1986.

Madhubuti, H. *Black Men: Obsolete, Single, Dangerous?* Chicago: Third World Press, 1989.

Moniz, D., and Bolton, W. "Fear of 'Acting White' Confines Blacks." *The State* (Columbia, S.C., newspaper), July 7, 1991, p. 1A.

Office of Vocational Education and Adult Education. *Adults in Transition: A Report on the Fourth Year of the Adult Education for the Homeless Program.* Washington, D.C.: Division of Adult Education and Literacy, U.S. Department of Education, May 1993.

Ogbu, J. U. "Literacy and Schooling in Subordinate Cultures: The Case of Black Americans." In D. B. Resnick (ed.), *Literacy in Historical Perspectives*. Washington, D.C.: Library of Congress, 1983.

Peterson, E. A. *Breaking the Bonds of Illiteracy in South Carolina: A Challenge for the Black Community. The State of Black South Carolina: 1995–1996. An Action Agenda for the Future.* Columbia, S.C.: Columbia Urban League, 1996.

Quigley, A. B. "Reasons for Resistance to Attending Adult Basic Literacy." In A. B. Quigley (ed.), *Understanding and Overcoming Resistance to Adult Literacy Education*. University Park, Pa.: Institute for the Study of Adult Literacy, 1995.

Woodson, C. G. *The Mis-Education of the Negro*. Trenton, N.J.: Africa World Press, 1990. (Originally published 1933.)

ELIZABETH A. PETERSON is assistant professor of adult and community education at the University of South Carolina, Columbia.

An exploration of the complex interaction of factors that shapes migrant adults' participation in Adult Basic Education programs leads to recommendations for effectively meeting migrant farmworkers' educational needs.

Voices from the Fields: Community-Based Migrant Education

Loida C. Velázquez

Traditionally, Adult Basic Education (ABE) and literacy programs have served individuals for whom schooling was an alienating experience. Fingeret (1985), Beder (1991), Quigley (1990, 1991, 1992), and Cervero and Kirkpatrick (1990) are among the ABE researchers who have examined the effects of negative attitudes about schooling on adults' literacy program participation. The theories and research findings of education theorists like Giroux (1983) and Ogbu (1990) have interpreted the ills of education and given meaning to the experiences of ABE learners and those who teach them.

Alienation can be defined as the perceived discrepancy between expectations for a role or activity and actual experience within that role or activity. Farnworth and Leiber (1989), for example, saw alienation resulting from the strain between a desired goal (such as upward mobility, money, the good life, steady employment, and a satisfying job) and the means to that goal (such as access to college or the acquisition in school of skills for a well-paying job). Seeman (1975) further defines alienation as a feeling of powerlessness, meaninglessness, and personal isolation. Although alienation from school is found across racial, ethnic, and gender groups, marginality is a common denominator. That is, alienated students are often members of linguistic or cultural groups that differ distinctively from the school's dominant culture.

This chapter examines the experiences of one such marginalized group: migrant farmworkers and their children. It situates migrants within a demographic and cultural context; examines migrant adults' perceptions of schooling, learning, and education—focusing on the example of one Hispanic migrant community and then turning to the literature for interpretation; and examines a successful ABE program designed for migrant adults and extracts recommendations for their effective education.

NEW DIRECTIONS FOR ADULT AND CONTINUING EDUCATION, no. 70, Summer 1996 © Jossey-Bass Publishers

Cultural and Social Context

Migrant workers are defined as agricultural laborers who travel within the geographical boundaries of the continental United States and Canada in pursuit of employment. They move along three identifiable streams: Eastern, Mid-Continent, and West Coast (King-Stoops, 1980). The Eastern stream is made up of Puerto Ricans, Mexican Americans, Anglos, Canadian Indians, and blacks, and flows mostly up and down the region east of the Appalachians. The Mid-Continent stream, composed of Mexicans, Mexican Americans, blacks, and more recently, Vietnamese and Cambodians, traces the Mississippi River basin. The West Coast stream is the largest movement, extending from California and Arizona to Oregon and Washington and composed primarily of documented and undocumented Mexicans, Central Americans, Vietnamese, Filipinos, and other Western Pacific immigrants.

Migrants are the most undereducated major subgroup in the United States, with a high school dropout rate larger than that of any other group (National Council of La Raza, 1990). Over 70 percent have not completed high school, and 75 percent are functionally illiterate (Hodgkinson, 1985). Their mobility, their language differences, and the cultural differences experienced as they move from one community to another combine with health and nutritional problems to negatively affect school achievement. The constant interruption of their educational process and the inability of schools to understand their culture and meet their needs lead to confusion, frustration, and a feeling of alienation that is a major factor in migrant students' dropping out of school.

A *culture* can be defined as a set of distinctive modes of behaving that are shared by a group. Migrant lifestyles revolve around working, moving on to find other work, and working again. The resulting behavioral patterns, "the culture of migrancy," have been observed throughout the three streams and reported independently by ethnographers examining people from different ethno-cultural backgrounds (Prewitt-Diaz, Trotter, and Rivera, 1990, p. 117). Hintz (1981), for example, studied a community of migrant workers in Ohio and described the migrant culture as follows:

> Migrant workers have a strong sense of family loyalty; respect for elderly persons; politeness; the children do not tease or "kid" an adult. They have pride for what they are and their heritage; maintain faith with the family and their religion. Migrant workers do not strive to obtain higher salaries and do not want more than they need. They consider their employers, and anglos generally, as "greedy," not satisfied, always wanting more. The migrant family stands firm in its values. They feel that diplomacy and tactfulness are very important in communicating with others. They are not demanding or aggressive towards agencies or employers. They are not likely to exert violent actions politically. [p. 13]

Although the ethnographic study by Prewitt-Diaz, Trotter, and Rivera (1990) focused on migrant children, it also increased our understanding of migrant families and their shared behavior patterns. Some of the patterns described in this study are outlined in the following paragraphs.

Gender roles. Marriage at a young age is common and typically signals the end of schooling, especially for females. There is enormous pressure for males to support the family and for females to have children. These complementary roles help young migrant couples survive but severely limit their chances for educational success and advancement. In most migrant communities, women are expected to both work in the fields and do household chores. Men and children are usually exempt from household responsibilities.

Adult and child roles. The age at which children begin to adopt adult roles differs across cultures. In many migrant families, boys begin to be treated as adults when, at age fifteen or sixteen, they can earn as much in the fields as their fathers. Girls start being treated as adults when they are capable of having children and managing a household. Most migrant children drop out of school once they are able to work in the fields and earn money. Because there is no tradition of mandatory education in their culture, migrant parents allow their children to decide whether or not to drop out of school once they are able to contribute to the family's sustenance. The difference between the role expectations of migrant families and those of the dominant society has serious consequences for educational programs.

Dealing with social institutions. Educational, health care, and social service agencies facilitate living in a complex society. One function of culture is to teach people how to best use this system of agencies. Migrants are often at a serious disadvantage because they do not understand the U.S. system. Some strive to be independent and take pride in meeting their family needs; others simply suffer in silence.

Powerlessness and the migrant cycle. Many migrants feel trapped in the cycle of migrancy. Their resulting belief that migrancy is their children's fate is sometimes misinterpreted as apathy by educational agencies.

Attitude toward authority. Although migrants have a generally positive attitude toward authority, their expression of this attitude is occasionally confusing to school personnel. For example, migrant parents trust the schools to know what is right for their children and feel that questions about the appropriateness of an educational program will be construed as a challenge to the teacher's authority and prestige.

Perceptions of Schooling, Learning, and Education

Perceptions are mental images we form based on our daily experiences and according to which we interpret the world. In my recent ethnographic study of a Hispanic migrant community in western North Carolina (Velázquez, 1993), migrant adults described a common perception of negative schooling experiences. The constant moving and the pressures to conform and to meet expectations proved to be a heavy burden. The schools, they felt, made no efforts to help them adjust. Many had to repeat grades and were left behind by age peers. Even those who were not turned off by school did not find encouragement there to discuss home problems. Others expressed open resentment of the insensitivity of teachers and administrators. All they remembered was the pain, rejection, and isolation—feelings that facilitated their decisions to drop out.

Schooling as a Painful Experience. Pain is not often discussed in educational circles, yet many recent ethnographic studies have given voice to experiences painfully engraved in dropout students' memories, students Quigley (1991) describes as "wounded by the schooling system" (p. 11). Along with their pain and rejection, the migrant adults in my study recall feeling powerless, personally isolated, and lacking control over the events affecting their school lives. The defensive response to school as a painful place is alienation. For these migrants, alienation was manifested in two ways: lack of connection with school processes and isolation. Ogbu (1990) blames the schools for such responses, observing that generations of minority students have been discouraged from investing time and effort in education and have dropped out or emotionally tuned out from their school classes.

Many of the migrants studied also talked about the many pressures they had to contend with: growing up poor, being in a family that was constantly moving, having to help with the care of younger siblings, and having to supplement the household income with outside work. Under these circumstances, school was seen as an extra pressure. Gibson (1993) found that immigrant students also view schooling with suspicion and ambivalence because it pressures them to conform to the dominant culture and to reject the values and beliefs of their culture. The student concludes that acquisition of skills valued by the dominant culture and acceptance of teacher authority and school rules are challenges that need to be resisted. Ogbu (1990) found that minority students, having historically been excluded from the high-quality education received by white students and consistently denied access to viable jobs, similarly resist the school culture. And in her study on urban adolescents, Fine (1986) concluded: "Whether dropping out is a personal act of rejection, assertion, joining one's peers, or giving up, it presumes a structural context that is being rejected, critiqued, and/or experienced as defeating by the actor" (p. 397).

School as a Meaningless Place. The view of school as a meaningless place is described often in the dropout research literature (Bishop, 1989; McLeod, 1987; Fordham and Ogbu, 1986). This meaninglessness arises when students do not see a connection between school and their personal futures—specifically, finding future jobs. For migrants and their children, the relationship between schooling and the future is particularly cloudy because many migrant families feel there is nothing they can do but farmwork. For the majority of those I interviewed, migrancy had become a family tradition. Some were fourth-generation migrant farmworkers, and some felt trapped because when they tried to do something else they were not paid as well. Moreover, because child labor laws allow thirteen-year-olds to do farmwork, children can make a significant contribution to the migrant family's household income, one that can make the difference between survival and despair, and a migrant family will view it as better for the immediate future of the whole family if the children join the adults in the fields. Thus, one reason school officials consider migrant labor a deterrent to education is that it gives youths access to money at an early age.

Dropping Out as an Accepted Solution to a Difficult Situation. Among migrants, dropping out from school is as much a family pattern as migrant farmwork. Most of my study participants had parents and siblings who were also migrant workers and who had dropped out of school at an early age. Of the migrant students in my study who had enrolled in a high school equivalency program between 1987 and 1990, 78 percent had dropped out of school between the seventh and ninth grades. They did so for a variety of reasons, and some were unique to the migrant lifestyle. Migrant youths in another study showed decreased self-esteem as grade level increased, reaching the lowest point at grade eight (Cranston-Gingras and others, 1993). The migrant family's decision to migrate is essentially a financial one, but its consequences include negative effects on social relationships, health, and educational opportunities.

In a survey by Apicella (1985), migrant dropout students gave the following reasons for leaving school: failing classes, did not like school, had very few credits for graduation, had to work, family needed money, did not feel a part of school, had problems with teacher, felt older than other students, got suspended and did not go back, and had problems with other students. Like Apicella, I found that migrants were dissatisfied with their early school experiences. Even though they consistently expressed a belief in the value of learning, they distrusted schools as means of improving employability and quality of life.

Dropping Out Is Not Synonymous with Rejection of Learning. Research examining nonparticipation in Adult Basic Education programs has traditionally focused either on school dropouts' psychosocial deficiencies or on deterrents to participation (Boshier, 1973; Hayes, 1989; Valentine and Darkenwald, 1990). However, in recent years, resistance theory has shifted the research focus to schooling's impact on students. Based on Marx's statement ([1867] 1969) that "every social process of production is at the same time a process of reproduction" (p. 531), radical educators have looked at school as an institution whose main function is the reproduction of the dominant ideology. Instead of blaming students for academic failure or nonparticipation, they blame the dominant society. More recent research has attempted to move beyond reproduction theories (Giroux, 1983) to emphasize the importance of human volition, struggle, and resistance to reproduction. Resistance theorists have attempted to demonstrate that the mechanism of social and cultural reproduction is never complete and always meets with partially realized elements of opposition. Quigley (1990, 1991, 1992), for example, found that undereducated adults resisted schooling in their earlier years and are now resisting Adult Basic Education programs for the same reasons. He concluded that they were not rejecting learning but schooling.

Although all the migrant adults I interviewed were school dropouts, they were active learners. They talked about street learning, showed pride in learning skills on their own, and told about their experiences in adult education programs. Indeed, most had tried to continue their education through traditional ABE and GED programs, but their initial contacts with such programs seemed to have been affected by their negative perceptions of schooling. It was only when they were recruited by a program especially designed for migrant adults that they were able to overcome these perceptions and view education as a means to better employment and personal satisfaction. All but one completed high school requirements once they found the appropriate program.

All the migrant adults made vivid and glowing comments about their belief in the value of education for themselves and their children. Though their parents had had little schooling and they themselves had not completed high school, most parents wanted their children to finish school. Some researchers have concluded that one difference between the values of dropout students and the values of the school system may be that these students value doing over mental activity and thus resist schooling when it no longer does what they value. Consequently, they might experience a greater sense of confidence and self-esteem after leaving school (Beder, 1991; Ziegahn, 1992). For many of these students, "learning can be embraced only after it has been mentally disassociated from formal education memories" (Ziegahn, 1992, p. 34).

Need for Alternatives to Traditional ABE Programs. "At the adult level, nothing will happen if we do not open opportunities and remove barriers for people whose motivational force to participate is low or negative" (Cross, 1981, p. 146). For adults who remain resisters, "school-based approaches to adult literacy are not likely to work, and, if we are to reach them, new approaches to adult literacy must be found" (Beder, 1991, p. 88). Yet most adult education programs continue to use the schooling model of teaching and the ideological goals of remedial education. When adults carry painful memories of schooling, they are not attracted to adult education programs that reproduce schooling models.

Curtis (1990) states that an empowered citizenry requires a definition of literacy that combines community development, traditional education, and social change. Curtis's proposed literacy for social change model integrates learning and community change and involves the following components: *fundamental skills*—the basic skills necessary for dealing with the written word; *critical thinking*—the capacity to understand and react to information; *cultural expression*—the realities of community life and people's joys, yearnings, struggles, and achievements expressed through music, drama, folklore, dance, and literature; and *individual/community action*—reflection upon personal and community problems and successes and the action arising from learning that is taken to address these issues. Variations of this model have been implemented by programs known as *community-based* or *popular education*.

Example of a Successful Learning Experience for Migrants

The unique High School Equivalency Program (HEP) has been praised by participants. Funded by the U.S. Department of Education to serve migrant and seasonal farmworkers exclusively, it was designed to meet their particular needs. The program schedule is flexible, giving students the opportunity to attend at their own convenience. The staff are bilingual teachers (English and Spanish) experienced in working with the migrant population. The program provides transportation and a stipend for incidental expenses. It is not curriculum driven but student centered, and its goal is to empower students through education and to assist them to become integrated into the local community.

The HEP project has been nationally recognized as a good example of a program for migrant adults. A further look at the factors contributing to the overall success of this program in reaching migrants reveals characteristics of effective adult education programs:

The program is geared to empower students by increasing their successful experiences, self-confidence, and feelings of self-worth and dignity.

Placement plans start at enrollment, and placement activities are geared to end in postsecondary education or competitive employment.

Class schedule is flexible, with a choice of morning, afternoon, or evening classes. Students unable to attend classes are allowed to take instructional material home, and instructors and counselors periodically check with those students either by phone or a home visit.

A strong promotion and recruitment program is maintained through visits to migrant gathering places such as laundromats, the migrant clinic, the Mexican store, the Spanish-speaking church, and the migrant housing section of town.

Coordinators, recruiters, counselors, and instructors are culturally and ethnically representative of the student body.

Bilingual counselors are available and an intensive personal and career counseling program is implemented.

An individually tailored educational and placement plan is developed, with the student leading the activity.

Staff receive regular training in adult education and culturally sensitive topics.

Teacher and program effectiveness are regularly evaluated by both staff and students.

Conclusion

Community-based adult education seems to be the appropriate vehicle for addressing the needs of a culturally diverse population, especially migrant farmworkers. The following recommendations are based on the belief that a successful adult education program depends to a great extent on how it responds to the cultural, political, socioeconomic, and experiential realities of the participants.

Research the target community and learn about its culture and its members' past schooling experiences.

Design the project around the goal of assisting participants to integrate into the local community. Assist the local community in learning about and receiving migrant farmworkers into its midst.

Provide an open and supportive environment and assist migrant farmworkers to overcome negative memories of schooling.

Build a strong network of community resources.

Offer classes that are flexible; involve migrant students in designing their own learning experiences.

Carefully select teachers and tutors who can serve as facilitators and are knowledgeable about participants' cultural norms.

Adopt instructional strategies based in group dialogue, personal interaction, and active participation. Design a curriculum that integrates learning basic skills with personal and community development activities.

Quigley (1992) states that "the decision to participate in literacy needs to be seen through the kaleidoscope of sociological influences, not the least of which is the impact of past schooling" (p. 211). Ethnographic studies seem to be the most appropriate way of unraveling the multiple influences on migrant adults' educational decisions. It is because migrants' early experiences of schooling, learning, and education have made a silent impact on their lives and continue to condition their attitudes and behaviors that adult education programs trying to reach migrants need to examine basic perceptions based on experience and the cultural context that gives them meaning.

References

Apicella, R. *Perceptions of Why Migrant Students Drop Out of School and What Can Be Done to Encourage Them to Graduate.* Oneonta: State University of New York at Oneonta, 1985.

Beder, H. *Adult Literacy: Issues for Policy and Practice.* Malabar, Fla.: Krieger, 1991.

Bishop, J. H. "Why the Apathy in America's High Schools?" *Educational Researcher,* 1989, *18,* 6–11.

Boshier, R. W. "Educational Participation and Dropout: A Theoretical Model." *Adult Education,* 1973, *23,* 255–282.

Cervero, R., and Kirkpatrick, T. "The Enduring Effects of Family Roles and Schooling on Participation in Adult Education." *American Journal of Education,* 1990, *99* (1), 77–94.

Cranston-Gingras, A., Platt, J., Flores, Y., Doone, P., and Martinez, Y. "Voices from the Field: What Research with Farmworker Children and Young Adults Is Telling Us." Paper presented at the National Conference on Migrant and Seasonal Farmworkers, Denver, Apr. 1993.

Cross, K. P. *Adults as Learners: Increasing Participation and Facilitating Learning.* San Francisco: Jossey-Bass, 1981.

Curtis, L. R. *Literacy for Social Change*. Syracuse, N.Y.: New Readers Press, 1990.

Farnworth, M., and Leiber, M. J. "Strain Theory Revised: Economic Goals, Education Means, and Delinquency." *American Sociological Review*, 1989, *54*, 263–274.

Fine, M. "Why Urban Adolescents Drop Into and Out of Public Schools." *Teachers College Record*, 1986, *87*, 393–409.

Fingeret, H. *North Carolina ABE Instructional Program Evaluation*. Raleigh: Department of Adult and Community College Education, North Carolina State University, 1985.

Fordham, S., and Ogbu, J. U. "Black Students' School Success: Coping with the 'Burden' of 'Acting White.'" *Urban Review*, 1986, *18*, 176–206.

Gibson, M. "Variability in Immigrant Students' School Performance: The U.S. Case." *The Social Context of Education Newsletter* (American Educational Research Association–Division G), Winter 1993, pp. 5–7.

Giroux, H. *Theory and Resistance in Education*. New York: Bergin & Garvey, 1983.

Hayes, E. R. "Hispanic Adults and ESL Programs: Barriers to Participation." *TESOL Quarterly*, 1989, *23* (1), 13–21.

Hintz, J. *Poverty, Prejudice, Power, Politics: Migrants Speak About Their Lives*. Columbus, Ohio: Avonelle, 1981.

Hodgkinson, H. L. *All One System: Demographics of Education Through Graduate School*. Washington, D.C.: Institute of Education Leadership, 1985.

King-Stoops, J. B. *Migrant Education: Teaching the Wandering Ones*. Bloomington, Ind.: Phi Delta Kappa Educational Foundation, 1980.

Marx, K. *Capital*. Moscow: Progress Publishers, 1969. (Originally published 1867.)

McLeod, J. *Ain't No Makin' It: Leveled Aspirations in a Low-Income Neighborhood*. Boulder, Colo.: Westview Press, 1987.

National Council of La Raza. *Hispanic Education: A Statistical Portrait*. Washington, D.C.: National Council of La Raza Publications, 1990.

Ogbu, J. U. "Minority Status and Literacy in Comparative Perspectives." *Daedalus*, 1990, *19* (2), 141–168.

Prewitt-Diaz, J. O., Trotter, R. T., and Rivera, V. A. *The Effects of Migration on Children: An Ethnographic Study*. Harrisburg, Pa.: Center de Estudios Sabre la Migración, 1990.

Quigley, A. B. "Hidden Logic: Reproduction and Resistance in Adult Literacy and Basic Education." *Adult Education Quarterly*, 1990, *40*, 103–115.

Quigley, A. B. "Looking Back in Anger: The Influences of Schooling on Illiterate Adults." Unpublished manuscript, 1991.

Quigley, A. B. "Resistance, Reluctance, and Persistence: Schooling and Its Effect on Adult Literacy." Paper presented at the Adult Education Research Conference, Saskatoon, Saskatchewan, 1992.

Seeman, M. "Alienation Studies." *Annual Review of Sociology*, 1975, *1*, 91–123.

Valentine, T., and Darkenwald, G. G. "Deterrents to Participation in Adult Education: Profiles of Potential Learners." *Adult Education Quarterly*, 1990, *41* (1), 29–42.

Velázquez, L. C. "Migrant Adults' Perceptions of Schooling, Learning, and Education." Unpublished doctoral dissertation, College of Education, University of Tennessee, 1993.

Ziegahn, L. "Learning, Literacy, and Participation: Sorting Out Priorities." *Adult Education Quarterly*, 1992, *43* (1), 30–50.

LOIDA C. VELÁZQUEZ is director of the Southeastern High School Equivalency Program, serving migrant and seasonal farmworkers and funded by the Office of Migrant Education of the U.S. Department of Education through the University of Tennessee, Knoxville.

An overview of correctional education in terms of its setting, problems, and successes reveals both commonalities and differences for educators of inmates to consider.

Prisons as Communities: Needs and Challenges

Waynne Blue James, James E. Witte, David Tal-Mason

"Prisons" . . . "penitentiaries" . . . "jails" . . . "correctional institutions"—these terms seem to conjure up the worst perceptions in the general public's mind of unrepentant criminals, escaping inmates, vicious killers, and repeat offenders. However, the majority of individuals convicted and sentenced to time in penal institutions will not repeat their offenses (Hirschi, 1986). The relationship between society and its penal system is often more a matter of perception than reality. Many reports deal with the costs, overcrowding, prison escapes, and policies and procedures that baffle the ordinary citizen. Few reflect the correctional system's successes. Educational efforts and the teaching of community-based literacy within the correctional system are crucial. This chapter examines the context of correctional education, describes the problems and constraints that impinge upon the successful delivery of correctional education programs, and outlines some current programs. We must understand that "what happens to offenders when they are in prison will eventually contribute to an increase or decrease in crime once they are again on the outside" (Sull, 1996, p. 6).

In 1994, the total number of prisoners under the jurisdiction of federal or state correctional authorities was 1,053,738 (Beck and Gilliard, 1995). Over 55 percent were located in ten states, with California, Texas, New York, and Florida accounting for 30 percent of the national inmate population. Federal taxpayers spend more per year to incarcerate one inmate ($20,804) than is spent on educating one child ($5,421) (Bureau of Justice Statistics Clearinghouse, 1996). Unfortunately, "while the incarcerated offender population has increased, the number and range of rehabilitative programs in adult correctional institutions often has decreased" (Wolford, 1989, p. 358).

More than 90 percent of all inmates will be released to continue their lives in society (Ryan and McCabe, 1993, 1994). Yet the educational level of most inmates is well below the national average (Clear and Cole, 1993; Kerka, 1995; Wolford, 1989). Only 33 percent have completed high school, compared to 85 percent of nonprisoners between the ages of twenty and twenty-five (Clear and Cole, 1993). These facts explain why providing adequate educational and vocational skills to this population is crucial. As Wolford (1989) says, "educators provide one of the few positive change-oriented programs available to inmates" (p. 357). Adult educators must strive to increase the likelihood that inmates will *not* repeat their offenses and will be successfully reintegrated into the community.

Context of Correctional Education

The context of prison education is first and foremost shaped by public philosophy about prison function. Today, despite the value of education to inmates, a punitive view of prison's purpose threatens to undermine the success of the available educational programs.

Historically, correctional education progressed from little more than chaplains teaching inmates in their cells to formal support by the American Correctional Association Congress in 1870. From 1870 to the creation of the Federal Bureau of Prisons in 1930, limited support for prison education existed. During the 1940s and the 1950s, incarcerated individuals received scant public attention, but the 1960s saw an increase in educational interest, efforts, and funds for inmates, and Ryan and McCabe (1994) called the 1970s the "Golden Age of correctional education" (p. 451). The philosophy of rehabilitation replaced the philosophy of punishment, and correctional education thrived and expanded. The modest gains realized in the 1960s and 1970s were in large part reversed, however, during the 1980s and 1990s.

The 1980s were characterized by conflict and confusion: conflict between the idea of rehabilitating the prisoner and the emphasis on crime control, confusion over the value of punitive treatment versus humanitarian action. Simultaneously, cutbacks in funding decreased the educational programs offered. So far, the 1990s have been marked by intense public pressure to punish those incarcerated, in the apparent belief that "getting tough" on criminals may decrease the incidence of crime. Strong opposition continues to any suggestion of inmates' receiving goods and services not available to law-abiding citizens, and to so-called country-club prisons. In actuality, there is no prisoner who would compare the restrictions of a correctional institution to the atmosphere of a country club.

Understanding the context of correctional education also lies in recognition of the distinctions among correctional facilities. *Prisons*, for the most part, are federal or state operated; *jails* typically are administered at the county level (although several states do not distinguish between county- and state-administered systems, Beck and Gilliard, 1995). Length of sentence determines the facility: individuals waiting for their cases to be heard or sentenced to less than one year are typically held in jails. The federal prison system consists of a range of institutions: detention centers, medical centers, prison camps, metropolitan correctional centers, and penitentiaries, which manage all persons "charged with or convicted of offenses against the United States" (Clear and Cole, 1993, p. 240). The various branches of the military also operate additional smaller detention centers and confinement facilities.

Most correctional institutions for men are classified by level of security (Clear and Cole, 1993, pp. 247–248). Maximum security institutions (about 26 percent of inmates) are designed to prevent escapes and to prevent inmates from hurting each other. Typically surrounded by towers and high walls, they have "strict limitations on the freedom of inmates and visitors." Medium security institutions (about 49 percent of inmates) generally resemble maximum security facilities, but greater emphasis is often placed on work and rehabilitation programs and "restrictions on inmates and visitors are less rigid than in facilities for more dangerous offenders." Minimum security facilities (about 25 percent of inmates) have more relaxed surveillance and "permit inmates and visitors as much freedom as is consistent with the concept of incarceration." Because female inmates are much fewer in number than male inmates, only one facility security level typically exists; however, they are housed in segregated levels within each facility. Female correctional facilities do present some different characteristics for educators to consider, although that discussion is beyond the scope of this chapter.

The type of institution and the designated level of security are crucial considerations when developing literacy programs. They determine what programs can be offered at an institution and what methods and materials can be used in classrooms. Inmate demographic and individual characteristics are also important elements in designing correctional education, affecting the learning experiences the instructor designs.

Despite minor percentage changes, the basic profile of the typical inmate has remained fairly constant over time (Beck and Gilliard, 1995). When prison inmates are categorized by type of offense, 45 percent are incarcerated for violent offenses, 22 percent for property offenses (for example, burglary, fraud, larceny, embezzlement), 26 percent for drug offenses, and 7 percent for public-order offenses (relating to, for example, immigration, weapons, escapes, and tax crimes).

About 95 percent of all inmates are male. Blacks account for 44 percent of the inmate population; whites, 35.8 percent; Hispanics, 17.6 percent; and "other," 2.6 percent (Beck and Gilliard, 1995). Inmates younger than eighteen years of age account for 1 percent of the prison population; those aged eighteen to twenty-four, 21 percent; twenty-five to thirty-four, 46 percent; thirty-five to forty-four, 23 percent; forty-five to fifty-four, 7 percent; fifty-five to sixty-four, 2 percent; and over sixty-five, 1 percent (Clear and Cole, 1993).

The educational profile, as suggested earlier, is bleak. Within state correctional custody, 65 percent of inmates lack a high school diploma (Clear and Cole, 1993), and 19 percent have an education of 8th grade or less. Only 22 percent are high school graduates, and an additional 12 percent have some college or a degree. In the state of Florida alone, 69.9 percent of the current inmate population tested at the 8th-grade level or below on the Tests of Adult Basic Education (TABE). Fully 36.9 percent were at the 5th-grade level or below. In addition, inmates include a "disproportionate number of unemployed, undereducated, and learning-handicapped individuals" (Wolford, 1989, p. 356). Given these figures, the importance of teaching literacy skills to inmates becomes apparent. Educational programs within the correctional system are vital links to the outside world and can lead to successful reintegration of the inmate into society. Community-based support, as discussed later, is also crucial to this successful reintegration. In addition, Ryan and McCabe claim that "prisons are safer for staff, offenders, and visitors if inmates are productively engaged in literacy training that promotes mental and physical health" (1994, p. 460).

The concept of community-based approaches to literacy programs, as addressed in this chapter, can be viewed from three separate, yet related, perspectives: the prison culture as viewed from an inmate's perspective; programs based in the community (largely for minimum security settings), where the inmates actually attend classes outside the correctional institution's walls, and prison-based programs, where the community is brought into the institution. Most staff educators serve as a bridge between the community and the institution. Because programs based outside the institution's walls are not as germane to this chapter, only the prison culture and prison-based programs are discussed here.

Further Challenges in Correctional Education

It is within this context of the prison setting that correctional educators seek to educate, train, and prepare inmates for a return to a society that has at least once rejected them, and "the prison educator's challenge is compounded by the uniqueness of prison culture: routines such as lock-downs and head counts, inmates' hearings and meetings with lawyers, all disrupt regular classes" (Sheather, cited in Kerka, 1995, p. 3). In addition to the contexts just discussed, educators need to recognize the impact and influence of the prison culture on inmates' participation in and receptivity to education. Collins and Niemi (1989), too, contend that "the challenge . . . is to create and sustain within this very restricting environment an adult education endeavor that will not be completely undermined by the multitude of frustrations and problems that are bound to arise" (p. 194).

Hence, it is of "vital importance" that prison education programs "be tailored to the prison culture" (Kerka, 1995, p. 4). Prison culture has its own norms, mores, group expectations, and individual practices; unique and complex, it differs dramatically from society as a whole. When inmates enter jail or prison, they experience an abrupt loss of freedom that dramatically terminates their previous life experience within that larger society. Elimination of the cultural and social bounds of the "outside culture" creates a void that tends to be filled by the institutional culture. According to Sykes (Santamour, 1987, p. 117), prisoners tend to shape the internal prison community so it can replace aspects of the society from which they have been removed. To view the prison simply as a structure housing "undesirables" and protecting society from criminals ignores the complexity of the correctional institution.

Prison as a Community: An Inmate's Perspective

From the inmate's perspective, the prison is a community. Strange as it may seem to an outsider, life goes on within the prison's walls and wires. Alliances are formed among *homeboys* and *homegirls* (people from one's hometown), *roaddogs* (those one knows from other prisons), roommates, coworkers, and members of one's race, ethnicity, or sexual orientation. The type of crime a prisoner has or has not committed determines his place in the community as much as his religious affiliation or shared interests. But the strongest alliances in prison form within each of the two most obvious social groups: *us* and *them*.

Prisoners make a basic distinction between those they snore with, eat with, and suffer beside, and those who order them about or lock them in. There are prisoners (us), and there are police (them).

Among prisoners, in addition, there are two basic classes: *convicts* and *inmates*. Convicts play a tight-lipped, stubborn, James Cagney sort of role. They disdain authority, wink at others' wrongdoing, and aid their homeboys in a fight. Inmates, in contrast, are motivated to get out of prison. They involve themselves in programs that might hasten their release. As a secondary goal, they attempt to increase their academic or vocational skills. Inmates submit to authority, comply with most of the rules, and struggle for officials' trust and respect—to the convicts' chagrin. Although inmates are likely to find literacy programs attractive, convicts regard them with contempt. Going to school just because "they" say you should is an act of treason or cowardice, and a decent convict will make no bones about it. Social pressures from convicts are much stronger than those from correctional educators. Convicts *live* with the prisoners that educational staff seek to teach and wield power over. How comfortable these potential students will find themselves during their time out of the classroom, the rest of their days and nights, is determined by the social pressures they experience within the prison.

The key to enhancing prisoners' participation in literacy programs, then, lies in getting to the convict. Lure the tough guys in, instill enthusiasm for educational goals, and make them each other's accomplices in literacy. Along with each convict comes one less enemy, and one more advocate that other convicts will listen to.

Prisons are communities and need to be approached as systems. No corrections student arrives in a vacuum. Ultimately, prisoners must take responsibility for their own education—because correctional education is an "inside job."

Other issues affect the development of educational programs for individuals who are members of the prison community. Materials often present problems for prison educators. Clear and Cole (1993), for example, state that "prison budgets seldom have the flexibility to permit the purchase of specialized educational aids, so the education programs often have to make do with inadequate, outdated, largely ill-suited materials" (p. 360). Kerka (1995) also identifies such problems and constraints as overcrowding, inadequate facilities, surroundings poor in verbal and sensory stimuli, peer pressure that discourages attendance or achievement, punitive philosophical approaches within particular institutions, and students who have negative early school experiences, lack of self-confidence, and poor attitudes about education. In addition, "the needs of adult prisoners differ from those of youthful students. Their attention span is different, their life/experience much broader, their sophistication greater" (Clear and Cole, 1993, p. 360).

Finally, educators should consider that instead of "viewing literacy as the inculcation of basic skills, embedding it in a broader perspective of education might address the hopelessness and powerlessness that may be both the cause and effect of inmates' actions before, during, and after incarceration" (Kerka, 1995, p. 4). To develop effective programs, educators should understand not only the prison culture and community, but the culture and the events that led the inmates to their particular situations.

All these cultural issues and constraints present unique challenges to the educator seeking to provide opportunities for inmates to better their own situation.

Current Prison Literacy Efforts

Regardless of location, prison education programs seem to have a similar focus of effort—improving the literacy skills of offenders with an eye to their successful reintegration into society. Jenkins, Steurer, and Pendry (1995, p. 23) assert that "educational attainment while in prison does seem to make a difference in the lives of incarcerated persons when they return to the community" (see also, for example, Newman, Lewis, and Beverstock, 1993; Morin, 1981; Porporino and Robinson, 1982; Werner, 1990).

Responsible Inmate-Taught Education (RITE) is an intensive twelve-week training program in Florida that prepares a prison system's better-educated inmates to serve as supplemental classroom teachers for the lower-level inmates. Discussions with the RITE graduates have indicated this program's exceptional impact on their self-concept and their greater sense of responsibility for not only their own education but also that of others. The program seems to be a positive influence on the community of inmates. Inmates being taught by the RITE graduates have expressed continuing appreciation that someone who "really knows what it's like on the inside" is providing instruction directly related to the situation at hand.

Ristow and Edeburn (1988) developed an inmate training program that integrated academic skills, life skills, and vocational training. Prior to the project, educational programs were independent of other programs within the prison. Inmates participating in the new integrated curriculum enjoyed a higher success rate in vocational training than did those trained prior to the new program.

Education programs for jail populations are often cut back due to the perception of many facility administrators that the relatively short period of incarceration gives inmates little opportunity to benefit from educational services. A second encumbrance to effective jail education programs is facility overcrowding. Since 1980, the nation's incarcerated population has more than doubled. On December 31, 1994, the number of sentenced prisoners per 100,000 U.S. residents was 387—up from 139 in 1980 (Beck and Gilliard, 1995). Administrators now concentrate on overcrowding issues while "paying less attention to in-jail programs aimed at dealing with illiteracy, drug and alcohol abuse, unemployment, mental illness, and dysfunctional families—problems that are characteristic of jail populations" (Smith and Silverman, 1994, pp. 414–415).

To gain insight into the effectiveness of short-term jail education programs, Smith and Silverman (1994) researched a program called INVEST, in Hillsborough County, Florida. The program goals for INVEST were to increase inmates' literacy levels, develop their personal sense of motivation and satisfaction, cultivate their desire for increased knowledge, increase their future employability, and ultimately reduce their recidivism. One unexpected research result was that the negative attitudes toward education often assumed to be typical of offenders were not supported by the findings. Instead, the results led to the opposite conclusion: inmates had positive attitudes toward education. This information is particularly noteworthy because administrators are more likely to allocate resources to programs that motivate participant support. Overall, Smith and Silverman concluded that INVEST "is innovative and challenging, and it allows students to work at their own pace without fear of embarrassment and exposure of their education inadequacies to other students in the class" (p. 430).

Laubach Literacy Action (1994) has identified what it considers some of the more exemplary prison-based but community-sponsored literacy programs. These programs encompass the range of possibilities from inmate-sponsored tutor programs to community-supported volunteer activities to institutionally funded approaches. Materials specifically aimed at reintegrating inmates into society are also becoming available from several sources. For example, Sull (1990, 1995) has written books that directly address some of the concerns discussed here. Wimer (1990) has developed a handbook that considers the specifics of working with releasees and probationers.

In correctional institutions, most educational programs have commonly accepted goals that include providing inmates with basic academic and vocational skills, an opportunity to change personal behavior and values, and a means of reducing the chance of reoffending. In addition, these educational programs meet institutional goals by providing passive control of inmate behavior, supporting the operational needs of the correctional institution, and providing institutional work assignments (Wolford, 1989).

Future Needs

Correctional institutions offer an opportunity to learn. The crux of the issue is not *whether* inmates will learn but rather *what* they will learn. If the corrections environment fails to support the acquisition of socially acceptable skills, then the inmate will acquire socially unacceptable skills and, essentially, emerge a better criminal. This continuing downward spiral is a disservice and an ever-increasing burden to society. The crucial need within correctional education, therefore, is to educate inmates to a level where each individual has the necessary literacy and vocational skills to function successfully in today's society. Community-based literacy programs, in particular, are a means of encouraging the socialization, or resocialization, of convicted inmates. Obviously, a variety of programs are needed to assist inmates' transition back into society; however, without the prerequisite skills for social success, inmates' chances of being reincarcerated increase.

Wolford (1989) comments on the need for correctional educators to consider a variety of educational program issues in the future, including mandatory versus voluntary program participation; opportunities for learning-handicapped offenders; linkages between industrial, training, and education programs; gender equity in education; assistance for inmates during reintegration into society; and program evaluation.

Ryan and McCabe (1994) forcefully warn that "the concept of merely caging offenders must be replaced by the concept of educating offenders. Jails, prisons, and reformatories must provide education and training to prepare offenders for return to society as productive, responsible, socially acceptable, economically self-sufficient, law abiding citizens" (p. 460).

"Successful prison literacy programs are *learner centered,* [and] recognize different learning styles, cultural backgrounds, and multiple literacies" (Kerka, 1995, p. 4). Successful programs are also participatory—educators recognize and use learners' strengths to shape their learning. Literacy efforts must be expressed in meaningful contexts that address individual learner needs by providing "engaging topics which motivate and sustain learner interest" (p. 4). Material written by inmates provides subjects that are relevant and serves as a model for others. Literacy programs that involve the entire family help inmates to perceive themselves in roles distinct from that of a prisoner.

Resource problems caused by overcrowding, inadequate facilities, outdated equipment, and minimal materials must be overcome creatively. Inventive class scheduling and broader definitions of classroom space (for example, meeting outdoors) can temporarily alleviate overcrowding. Maintaining good relations with the prison administration and local educational establishments can go a long way toward upgrading classroom facilities and equipment, as can educating oneself concerning alternative resources, such as grant monies and tax-deductible donations.

Conclusion

Although the topic of correctional education generally elicits as many opinions as there are discussants, adult education remains a valuable tool in decreasing crime. Individuals who commit crimes against society are generally lacking the skills necessary to become part of that society. The choices are relatively simple: send criminals to prison to hone their illicit skills or replace those skills with knowledge and abilities that will permit successful social integration.

The vital importance of social integration can best be illustrated by inmates who say, "The sentence starts when I walk out the main gate" (Sutton, 1992, p. 51). Once released, inmates face serious problems—surviving economically, finding a place to live, and being accepted as a member of the at-large society. Community-based prison literacy programs can assist this transition in several crucial ways; by providing basic educational and vocational skills and by preventing inmates from becoming so institutionalized that they are unable to adapt to their communities upon release.

Sull (1996) declares that "education is the ultimate weapon against crime, and the public and politicians must embrace this" (p. 6). Correctional education is not being soft on crime or making life easy on the criminal. Correctional education is the only positive return on incarceration. As educators, we must meet the need for correctional education in terms of the highly rigorous specialty it has become. A failure to do so simply adds oil to the revolving door of corrections.

References

Beck, A. J., and Gilliard, D. K. Prisoners in 1994. Washington, D.C.: Bureau of Justice Statistics, U.S. Department of Justice, 1995.

Bureau of Justice Statistics Clearinghouse. [http://ncjrs.aspensys.com.81/ncjrshome.html]. 1996.

Clear, T. R., and Cole, G. F. American Corrections. (3rd ed.) Belmont, Calif.: Wadsworth, 1993.

Collins, M., and Niemi, J. A. "Advancing Adult Basic Education in Prisons." In S. Duguid (ed.), Yearbook of Correctional Education. Burnaby, Canada: Simon Fraser University, 1989.

Hirschi, T. "Presidential Address," presented to the American Society of Criminology, Atlanta, Nov. 1986.

Jenkins, H. D., Steurer, S. J., and Pendry, J. "A Post-Release Follow-Up of Correctional Education Program Completers Released in 1990–1991." Journal of Correctional Education, 1995, 46 (1), 20–24.

Kerka, S. Prison Literacy Programs. ERIC Digest no. 159. Columbus, Ohio: ERIC Clearinghouse on Adult, Career, and Vocational Education, 1995. (ED 383 859)

Laubach Literacy Action. Community-Based Prison Literacy Program Models. Syracuse, N.Y.: Laubach Literacy Action, 1994.

Morin, L. "Introduction: On Prison Education." In L. Morin (ed.), On Prison Education. Ottawa: Canadian Government Publishing Centre, 1981.

Newman, A. P., Lewis, W., and Beverstock, C. *Prison Literacy*. Philadelphia: National Center on Adult Literacy, 1993. (ED 363 729)

Porporino, F. J., and Robinson, D. "The Correctional Benefits of Education." *Journal of Correctional Education*, 1982, 43 (2), 92–98.

Ristow, R. S., and Edeburn, C. E. "Life Skills: Infusion of Curriculum at a Maximum Security Prison." *Adult Literacy and Basic Education*, 1988, 12 (2), 91–97.

Ryan, T. A., and McCabe, K. A. "The Relationship Between Mandatory vs. Voluntary Participation in a Prison Literacy Program and Academic Achievement." *Journal of Correctional Education*, 1993, 44 (3), 134–138.

Ryan, T. A., and McCabe, K. A. "Mandatory Versus Voluntary Prison Education and Academic Achievement." *The Prison Journal*, 1994, 74 (4), 450–461.

Santamour, M. B. "The Mentally Retarded Offender." In C. M. Nelson, R. B. Rutherford, Jr., and B. I. Wolford (eds.), *Special Education in the Criminal Justice System*. Columbus, Ohio: Merrill, 1987.

Smith, L. G., and Silverman, M. "Functional Literacy Education for Jail Inmates." *The Prison Journal*, 1994, 74 (4), 414–432.

Sull, E. C. *The Ex-Inmate's Complete Guide to Successful Employment*. Buffalo, N.Y.: Aardvark, 1990.

Sull, E. C. *Bars & Books: How to Successfully Reach & Teach Inmates*. Buffalo, N.Y.: Correctional Education, 1995.

Sull, E. C. Letter to the Editor. *Time*, Feb. 5, 1996, p. 6.

Sutton, P. *Basic Education in Prisons: Interim Report*. Hamburg, Germany: United Nations Educational, Scientific, and Cultural Organization, 1992. (ED 348 495)

Werner, D. R. *Correctional Education: Theory and Practice*. Danville, Ill.: Interstate, 1990.

Wimer, M. *Teaching the Hard-to-Reach: Working with Releasees and Probationers: A Handbook for Adult Educators*. Huntsville, Tex.: Education Service Center Region VI, 1990.

Wolford, B. I. "Correctional Facilities." In S. B. Merriam and P. M. Cunningham (eds.), *Handbook of Adult and Continuing Education*. San Francisco: Jossey-Bass, 1989.

WAYNNE BLUE JAMES *is professor of adult and vocational education, University of South Florida.*

JAMES E. WITTE *is a retired U.S. Army officer, corporate trainer, and doctoral candidate at the University of South Florida.*

DAVID TAL-MASON *is a Florida inmate who received his GED and associate's, bachelor's, and master's degrees during his nineteen years of incarceration and wrote the grant application for the Responsible Inmate-Taught Education program.*

A staff development project can be designed to help adult education teachers connect their classes and curriculum with the community.

Building Connections: Classrooms and Communities in Rural Virginia

Mary Beth Bingman, Marie Martin, Amy Trawick

Classrooms are communities and are in communities. This chapter discusses a project designed to help adult education practitioners build the strengths of the communities that are their classes while they work with students to explore, learn from, and change the communities where they live. The project is part of the Regional Adult Education Practitioners Training Project, developed to supplement Virginia's Baseline Training for adult education practitioners.

We began the project hoping to develop training that would enable teachers in adult education and literacy programs to incorporate community issues into their curricula, using participatory approaches like those developed by educators from grassroots groups. We wanted to discover if methods that came out of activist organizations could be used by teachers working in more traditional programs. Here, we describe the project context, how the project was designed and carried out, and the thoughts and reflections of trainers and teachers who were part of the project. Some implications of this kind of work and questions about this approach to literacy education conclude the discussion.

Community-Based Education in Ivanhoe

Southwest Virginia is a rural area of valleys and long ridges, of farming, small manufacturing, timbering, and in the "far" southwest, coal mining. Some counties are relatively prosperous; in many the economy is a major concern. Unemployment rates run as high as 16 percent (in November 1995, for example) in the coalfields ("Most Jobless Rates," 1995). Families have often lived in the same communities for generations, and the prospect of leaving to find work is difficult.

Ivanhoe is a small southwest Virginia town. After the town's last industry closed in 1981, community members organized the Ivanhoe Civic League, which worked to stop the proposed sale of a local industrial park and to recruit industry (Hinsdale, Lewis, and Waller, 1995). Its focus soon expanded from economic development to education, cultural programs, and a project that brings church and college volunteers to the community to learn about community development while they repair houses and help out in other ways. The education program has included GED and community college classes, an adult literacy program, and after-school tutoring. The league was able to hire its own adult education teacher/coordinator in 1992, someone who had come to Ivanhoe as a college volunteer and had stayed. Wanting to use materials and instructional approaches that came from the community and empowered students, he found support in the Community in the Classroom project, sponsored by the Center for Literacy Studies.

Community in the Classroom

The Center for Literacy Studies (CLS) at the University of Tennessee, Knoxville, was founded in 1988 with the goal of working with practitioners to bridge theory and practice in adult literacy. Teachers and learners participate in the center's work, which includes professional development, program development, evaluation, curriculum design, and research. CLS staff bring to their work a wide range of experience in activism, community development, and participatory research in the Appalachian region. Center approaches to education and research have been influenced by the work of Myles Horton (Horton and Freire, 1990; Horton, Kohl, and Kohl, 1990) and Paulo Freire (Freire, 1970; Freire and Macedo, 1987) and by a belief in the power of ordinary people to analyze and change their lives.

The Community in the Classroom project began in 1992, when CLS staff and members of ten grassroots community organizations met to explore ways to integrate adult education with their other work (Bingman and White, 1994; Merrifield, White, and Bingman, 1994), including economic development, housing rehabilitation, parenting education, emergency family support, preschools, and organizing to obtain clean water. Several of the organizations were already operating adult education and literacy programs, and all hoped to do so eventually.

Goals and Structure. Community in the Classroom goals are:

To build community inside the classroom by developing a community of teachers and learners who share decision making

To bring community into the classroom by building curriculum around community issues

To bring the classroom into the community by involving the group of learners in the work of community groups

To build a community of programs as a means of utilizing and learning from this approach.

Teams from each organization came together in a series of eight workshops over two years to share experiences and learn from each other. Topics included leadership development, building participation, developing curriculum around community issues, documentation, building strong organizations, and producing materials. The workshops were planned and facilitated by the participants, and each team worked in its own organization to implement what team members had learned. Participants learned a great deal, both about literacy and about the processes of building leadership and ownership in a group. The following section details one community's experience in the process.

Example. In Ivanhoe, education program coordinators used ideas from Community in the Classroom in various ways. In the following excerpt, Ivanhoe participant Michael Blackwell describes his learning.

Our [Community in the Classroom] experience had modeled the incremental development of a sense of responsibility in the learner by requiring the constituent groups to plan the workshops, host visitors, and determine the direction of the entire project, but with careful, non-oppressive support and guidance. For us, as practitioners, the process of being asked to take responsibility for the actual content and program of the training, allowed us to transcend the role that we usually define for ourselves in a training—"the trained." Which means that instead of sort of idly receiving knowledge, and occasionally being goaded into something resembling action and participation, we had to do things and make decisions.

Additionally we had to cooperate and plan with the other community groups, sometimes in small groups, sometimes in the whole group. The bottom line was that after a workshop, we were usually inspired to try something different. [Blackwell and Armbrister, 1993, p. 3]

One method used to initiate classroom ideas about community was a "topic of the month" approach to theme-based curricula. After a slow start, this approach blossomed and became powerful when a group of adult educators from Mali planned a visit to Ivanhoe, as Michael Blackwell describes:

The event that we prepared for was a week long visit by a group of community practitioners from Mali, Africa. The beauty of it was that the experience was of a type that people were very skilled at: the receiving of guests. [We] broke the whole issue into two basic parts and our group of seven students took it from there. We asked, "What do you want these people to learn about you?" and, "What do you want to learn about them?"

We spent the next four or five weeks inductively learning what culture is, through our exploration and discovery of our own history; by trying to figure out what would be important to them, we discovered what was important to us, and why. What different aspects of our culture did we want them to know about? Did we want them to see everything, warts and all? What are some of those warts anyway? What are our strengths, what are we proud of? These are the questions we asked of ourselves. By the students' originating and posing these questions, the discussion just really came out and people took a good, critical, analytic view of things, without prodding and in a way that we had never heard before.

The morning class decided on a tour of the Ivanhoe area. We sat down and brainstormed what places in Ivanhoe were important and why. We asked some of the older people in the community to go around with us and tell us what they knew. The students themselves also had a lot to say about their town. The tour was a huge success, and the morning students and the old folks all came back that evening for a community pot-luck supper. We ended up talking till the Malians were ready to pass out. We had the first public dialogue about culture and racism heard here in years. We talked about ways of life, families, women's issues, everything, and much of the conversation grew from the questions and short presentations that the evening class had formulated themselves. It was an awesome experience.

The students were enraptured, and it stimulated topics for a month. Each person wrote up their opinions and reflections of the event. The writing (having been preceded by a couple months of "at-ease" writing) went through peer editing and revision, so that by the time the pieces made it [into] the newsletter, they had been through about four revisions, and [were] strong. The people cared about what they had written, and had taken responsibility for the event and the issues that grew out of it. [Blackwell and Armbrister, 1993, pp. 3–4]

In 1994, funding for the Community in the Classroom project ended, but interest in the work continued in several communities. In Ivanhoe, the education coordinator explored obtaining Virginia Office of Adult Education funds to share the skills and ideas of Community in the Classroom with other southwest Virginia adult education teachers. This led to the Ivanhoe Civic League's participation in what became the Regional Adult Education Practitioners Training Project.

Regional Adult Education Practitioners Training Project

The federal Adult Education Act designates funds (known as "353" monies) for staff development and special demonstration projects. In 1994, members of the Western Highlands Regional Literacy Coordinating Committee, including staff from Wytheville Community College, New River Community College, Radford University, and the Ivanhoe Civic League wrote a project proposal that was funded by these 353 monies; and in 1995, the Regional Adult Education Practitioners Training Project began designing, field testing, and evaluating four staff development modules, or components, based on the Community in the

Classroom model. The modules were designed to supplement the Baseline Instructor Training Program used by the Virginia Office of Adult Education and the Adult Education Centers for Professional Development to introduce instructors to the Virginia adult learning system, to concepts of adult learning and development, and to methods and planning of instructional approaches. These modules are interactive and are often presented by trainer practitioners. They cover critical thinking, community resources and issues, workplace teaching, and teaching strategies for adults with learning disabilities. Each was designed by a team made up of a team leader and two adult education practitioners working under the supervision of one of the collaborating institutions.

The authors of this chapter were the development team for the component on integrating community issues into the classroom. Martin and Trawick were already using student concerns as topics for classroom work and came to the project with an interest in strengthening their classroom connections to the community.

Reflections on Developing Project Workshops

Our first team task was developing a shared understanding of what we were about. We held a series of meetings/workshops, trying out activities first in the meeting and then in our classes. We reflected on what had and had not worked and exchanged thoughts and reflections on the process and our goals. After trying a variety of activities, we organized what we had learned into two staff development workshops, described later.

Each of us experienced the developmental process somewhat differently.

Mary Beth Bingman. When I began working with the Ivanhoe Civic League to plan this project, I expected that the challenge would be getting participating teachers to adopt the exciting ideas and approaches presented. I felt that most of my work had already been done: activities had been developed; workshops had been designed. I would need only to make a few modifications. The reality was much more complex and much richer. As I planned my first meeting with the teachers on the team, I realized my thinking had changed.

After the Community in the Classroom project, I had participated in the institute Learner at the Center, working with Hanna Fingeret, from Literacy South, among others, in a course that focused on building adult literacy curricula with learners around their concerns and interests (Fingeret, 1989, 1993; King, Fingeret, McCullogh, and Estes, 1993). I drew from this work in designing processes used in the Virginia project. Teachers were involved both as participant learners and as practitioners analyzing the process. Instead of focusing on community needs defined by a grassroots organization, as in the Community in the Classroom project, we began with community needs defined by learners. This was consistent with the approach of Learner at the Center and the approach used by the other two team members.

Marie Martin. Making classroom connections with community issues sounded like an interesting concept when the idea originally was presented.

Because I live in Max Meadows, a small rural community similar to Ivanhoe, I had read about some of Ivanhoe's classroom-community cooperation, and my community has received guidance from Ivanhoe since the organization of its own civic league four years ago. In our staff development project, as Amy and I tried Mary Beth's ideas in classes with our adult learners, we reviewed, revised, and added to them, keeping in mind our objectives, which were to help adult learners get concerned with community issues, learn from each activity, and improve in reading, writing, sharing, and using math to help solve community problems.

My students became involved eagerly. They learned interesting things about each other, especially in activities centering on community maps (described later) and family trees. Each involvement deepened their interests in community themes and caused them to become more critical thinkers. In using this learning approach, I have become ever mindful of how a practitioner, as well as an adult learner, can gain from each endeavor. Through this project, my classes and I have gotten to know each other better, and we now have a better understanding of community issues.

Amy Trawick. When I heard about this project, I was intrigued. With changes afoot for the social services system, I had already made plans to encourage my adult students to become more active in their community—to find the power to affect what was happening to them and to others that they knew.

In the past, I had invited guest speakers from the community, and we had used current events as writing and discussion topics. So I was excited about finding other ways of plugging into the community. Yet as we began the project, I had two major concerns. First, I questioned what I thought to be a call to be a political agent. I did not want to organize some big *class project* to affect some big *issue*. I did not have the time or the inclination. Second, I questioned how my students, focused on preparing for the GED tests, would respond to time spent on material that did not directly relate to those tests.

Then, as we worked on finding themes that struck a chord with everyone in a class, I was afraid at first that I would not be able to find these commonalities. I did have some difficulty at first, but through dialogue an issue would naturally evolve. Using such techniques as community maps and paper quilts (described later), people in the class had the opportunity to talk about perceived community needs. For example, lack of recreational opportunities for youths emerged as a concern. Once that topic was decided upon, however, I wondered "now what?" We had an issue; what were we to do with it? But again, by keeping the conversation alive, the class arrived at an appropriate action—in this case, to invite a speaker who organizes programs for youth in our community.

The next steps unfolded as we went along. One of the hardest things for me as the "teacher" was not having a plan that showed where we were going from the very beginning. Once we identified a common concern, I then wanted the *class* to have a plan. Luckily, I realized that my students did not need or want to have this community stuff crammed down their throats. They needed time to think about their concerns, but they also needed time and encouragement to realize they *could* make a difference. For example, when we were brainstorming points we wanted to make to our speaker, the perception that "it won't matter what we tell him!" was expressed over and over. Yet at the end of that day's discussion, one woman pulled me aside and asked with more than a hint of hope in her voice, "Do you really think he'll listen?" It was clear that she and others were beginning to see the *possibilities* of what *might* happen because of their influence, and I felt that this was a tremendous first step for many of my students.

Finding their common threads of interest and being "allowed" to explore personal interests that evolved from class discussion motivated the students and enhanced many different types of learning. As a result, I came away with an understanding of the value of using community themes, but I also became more comfortable with dealing in-depth with *issues*, once I saw that we could *explore* an issue as a class and *act* on issues either as individuals or as a group. I also came away from the project comfortable with how community-focused learning would affect my serious GED students. Students set individual goals when they enroll in my class, and all small-group and class "lessons" are optional. I decided I would not take it as a personal affront if students chose to work in their books instead of participating. In reality, however, I found that the GED students were easily involved in these "new" lessons, perhaps because they were a change. They added a spark of enthusiasm for gaining knowledge of the community's leaders and resources.

Through our experience with the project, Marie and I learned about participatory curriculum development, and we did so in a participatory way. Because we experienced the type of training we would be providing, we were able to point out concerns, offer suggestions, and in effect, affect change—much in the same way as we would want our adult education students to do. I was able to experience the value of participatory learning—the motivation of ownership—and to desire it for the members of my own class.

Workshop Design

The original Community in the Classroom project had included eight day-long workshops held over nearly two years. Due to time and funding constraints, the Regional Adult Education Practitioners Training Project components were structured as two four-hour sessions. Although this meant that the workshops we developed and piloted were more intense than we might have wished, we were able to include both practical activities and opportunities for participants to reflect on the theory and implications of using learner-centered and participatory approaches.

Nine teachers and administrators from Adult Basic Education and literacy programs in southwest Virginia participated in the pilot workshops. In the first workshop, participants were to take part in a series of small-group activities to identify common interests that could be developed as curriculum themes. We wanted to build a sense of community among the participants and have them practice identifying the common concerns or themes.

After introductions, we began with paper quilt, an activity that elucidates commonalities in a group and resonates with local culture. On four colored sheets of paper, each person wrote four or five words about himself or herself and his or her family, class, and community. People shared their responses in small groups and then created the paper quilt by taping their papers on the wall in a pattern they had designed. The next activity also enabled people to come to know each other and determine commonalities, but it focused on the community as a geographical, political, social, and economic space. Working on newsprint, each person drew a map of his or her community's political, geographical, economic ("where people work or go to buy"), and/or social aspects as he or she chose to define them. The participants shared the maps in their small groups and displayed them next to their quilts. Then, still in the small groups, participants identified common themes.

After a break, we introduced writing and prewriting activities as a way to identify common concerns or themes. Using activities drawn from *Making Meaning, Making Change* (Auerbach, 1992), *Many Literacies* (Gillespie, 1990), and *The Jellico Handbook* (Lewis and Gaventa, 1988), participants shared their work and identified themes they had in common.

We introduced participatory curriculum development by having the group read a passage from Auerbach (1992) answering the question, "So what is participatory curriculum development?" Next the group read *Heart to Heart*, a curriculum sample published by Literacy South (Rose and Ellrich, 1993), and identified its elements of participatory curriculum. For example, Auerbach's criterion that the content of a participatory curriculum come from the learners' social context was clearly evident in *Heart to Heart* when a class of older adults studied the health risks affecting heart disease.

We closed the first workshop by analyzing the process we had used. We asked participants to recollect each activity, consider why we had used that activity, identify the basic skills that were developed, and suggest ways the activity could be extended. Group members found that we had used the paper quilt activity to find common bonds, to generate information or data, and as a small-group activity. They thought they had developed skills in categorization, vocabulary, working in small groups, and consensus building. They suggested extending activities by analyzing the parts of speech used as descriptors and by using quilt making to teach math and geometry.

The second workshop, held two weeks later, was directed to activities of reflection and discussion of theoretical concerns. After a focusing activity, the participants shared how they had used activities from the first workshops with their classes, and reflected on what had happened and what they had learned.

In order to examine various philosophical approaches to adult literacy education, the participants had been asked to read an excerpt from *It Belongs to Me,* in which Fingeret (1993) uses Lytle and Wolfe's framework (1989) to help practitioners clarify their philosophy. Lytle and Wolfe suggest that liter-

acy can be viewed in multiple ways: as a set of skills, as the ability to do particular tasks, as the capacity to take part in specific social or cultural practices,
and as the ability to take part in critical reflection and action.

Recording responses on a chart, we asked participants to think about
these four approaches to literacy. First, we asked them to think how they used
each form of literacy in their own lives. Most of their uses of literacy were in
social and cultural practices. Next, we asked them how they approached literacy in their classes. In contrast to their own reported use of literacy, they asked
their students to use literacy in the practicing of skills and work on isolated
tasks. Their charted responses made it clear that they used literacy in one way
but taught it in another. As a result, we spent some time discussing not only
how literacy could be practiced in an authentic context in classes but also how
community issues and concerns could be used in all approaches to literacy. We
also listed a variety of community materials that could be used. Marie Martin
gave an example of how she had used a community issue in the past week with
her class. Class members had read a newspaper article that announced a hearing on new industry in the county. They then listed economic development
possibilities for their county and classified list items as recreational, agricultural, business, medical, industrial, and educational. Working together, they
wrote a letter to the development authority, which was subsequently read at
the hearing.

The other major section of the second workshop examined problem-
posing education. The group had read the article "Using Problem-Posing Dialogue in Adult Literacy Education" (Nixon-Ponder, 1995) at home. We practiced
this approach, using an issue identified in the first workshop: participants' concerns about the changes occurring in their communities. The facilitators did a
skit that presented three viewpoints on change that served to pose the problem.
We then talked about how the problem might affect the participants personally,
the various factors that lead to community changes, and possible solutions or
alternatives. Next, we asked participants to switch roles and to think as teachers, and we facilitated their consideration of the ways they could build curriculum from a similar kind of problem-posing exercise in their own classrooms.

The training workshop wound down with a brief discussion of how one's
philosophical perspective on literacy affects the assessment approach one uses.
The workshop concluded with facilitator and participants talking together
about the participants' plans and concerns regarding the implementation of
what they had learned. We also asked for a final written evaluation.

Conclusion

As a result of this initial training in which nine practitioners participated, we
know that a few of the activities presented are being used in participants' classes.
The teachers on the design team have gone a good deal farther and are building curriculum units around community issues and concerns as identified by
their students.

At this time, concrete conclusions about project outcomes would be somewhat premature. Nevertheless, one finding does seem apparent. We began this process hoping to discover whether the approaches developed by practitioners active in community-based organizations could and would be used by practitioners in public and private programs whose focus is individual education rather than community development and change. Our answer is a tentative yes, based on the following information: the written evaluations from the two workshops were quite positive, participants particularly liked the nonprint activities, and they also commented that they had learned new facilitation skills and ways to identify community themes. What is not as clear is how the participants will implement community connections in their adult education programs. From the oral and written feedback we received, it seems likely that people will try various activities and will make greater use of community topics and issues in their work. It is not clear that they will actually build their curricula around community issues or how much students will be involved. This is not to say that these things will not happen, only that the outcome is not clear at this point.

Although we cannot draw firm conclusions, we have seen several implications—for content, for assessment, and for training and support for teachers of adult education and literacy programs. From workshop discussions and the work the team teachers did in their own classes, it seems clear that practitioners see the value in using community issues as content and are able to use this material to build curriculum. We also began a discussion of assessment, and at least those who had worked with portfolios were able to envision how learning from curricula built around community themes might be assessed.

However, as was pointed out to us over and over, all this takes time—time for preparation, time for follow-up. To implement this kind of curriculum development process, teachers need the paid planning time that is rarely part of their jobs. To expect teachers to build community-connected curricula with their students without supported planning time is both unrealistic and disrespectful. In addition, we found that while the teachers on the original design team had time not only to plan but to develop ideas, with a venue for support and feedback, it was difficult to build this kind of time into two four-hour workshops. For the team teachers, as for the original Community in the Classroom participants, participation in planning workshops supported their ability to implement community issues in their own classes. This kind of implementation and reflection over time may be the essential support needed if teachers are to implement such a challenging change in practice. A third way time may be a factor is that students may resist spending time away from their "real" studies. Trawick's experience, described earlier, indicates that this may not be the case, however.

This project also has also raised questions about power and action. What does it mean for a teacher to give up power in the classroom? Is it the role of adult education teachers and students to act in the community? These are questions Trawick dealt with in her earlier reflections and that were raised in our workshops. We do not have definitive answers but tend to agree with the training participant who wrote: "It will only enhance our community to increase involvement by folks who have traditionally lacked strong voices."

References

Auerbach, E. *Making Meaning, Making Change: Participatory Curriculum Development for Adult ESL Literacy*. Washington, D.C.: Center for Applied Linguistics, 1992.

Bingman, M. B., and White, C. "Appalachian Communities: Working to Survive." In J. Hautecoeur (ed.), *Alpha 94: Literacy and Cultural Development Strategies in Rural Areas*. Toronto: Culture Concepts, 1994.

Blackwell, M., and Armbrister, A. *Final Report: ACBE. From the Ivanhoe Civic League Inc. Re: The Community in the Classroom Project, 1992–1993*. Unpublished report. Washington, D.C.: Association for Community Based Education, 1993.

Fingeret, A. "The Social and Historical Context of Participatory Literacy Education." In A. Fingeret and P. Jurmo (eds.), *Participatory Literacy Education*. New Directions for Adult and Continuing Education, no. 42. San Francisco: Jossey-Bass, 1989.

Fingeret, H. *It Belongs to Me: A Guide to Portfolio Assessment in Adult Education Programs*. Durham, N.C.: Literacy South, 1993.

Freire, P. *Pedagogy of the Oppressed*. New York: Seabury Press, 1970.

Freire, P., and Macedo, D. *Literacy: Reading the Word and the World*. New York: Bergin & Garvey, 1987.

Gillespie, M. *Many Literacies: Modules for Training Adult Beginning Readers and Tutors*. Amherst, Mass.: Center for International Education, 1990.

Hinsdale, M. A., Lewis, H., and Waller, M. *It Comes from the People: Community Development and Local Theology*. Philadelphia: Temple University Press, 1995.

Horton, M., and Freire, P. *We Make the Road by Walking: Conversations on Education and Social Change* (B. Bell, J. Gaventa, and J. Peters, eds.). Philadelphia: Temple University Press, 1990.

Horton, M., Kohl, J., and Kohl, H. *The Long Haul: An Autobiography*. New York: Doubleday, 1990.

King, J., Fingeret, H., McCullogh, P., and Estes, J. *It Brought a Richness to Me: A Resource Manual for Participatory Literacy Practitioners*. Durham, N.C.: Literacy South, 1993.

Lewis, H. M., and Gaventa, J. *The Jellico Handbook: A Teacher's Guide to Community-Based Learning*. New Market, Tenn.: Highlander Center, 1988.

Lytle, S., and Wolfe, M. *Adult Literacy Education: Program Evaluation and Learner Assessment*. Columbus: Center on Education and Training for Employment, Ohio State University, 1989.

Merrifield, J., White, C., and Bingman, M. B. "Community in the Classroom: Literacy and Development in a Rural Industrialized Region." In J. Hautecoeur (ed.), *Alpha 94: Literacy and Cultural Development Strategies in Rural Areas*. Toronto: Culture Concepts, 1994.

"Most Jobless Rates, Number of Jobs Down in Coalfields." *The Coalfield Progress*, Dec. 12, 1995, p. 2.

Nixon-Ponder, S. "Using Problem-Posing Dialogue in Adult Literacy Education." *Adult Learning*, 1995, 7 (2), 10–12.

Rose, R., and Ellrich, T. *Heart to Heart: A Learner Centered Curriculum Sample*. Durham, N.C.: Literacy South, 1993.

MARY BETH BINGMAN is associate director at the Center for Literacy Studies, University of Tennessee, Knoxville, and was a Community in the Classroom coordinator.

MARIE MARTIN is lead teacher, Mt. Rogers Regional Adult Education Program, Wytheville, Virginia.

AMY TRAWICK is lead teacher, Jefferson Adult Education class, Pulaski, Virginia.

Is there a rationale for incorporating health materials in literacy programs? Current data say yes, and innovative models of implementation are promising.

Literacy and Health Communities: Potential Partners in Practice

Peggy A. Sissel, Marcia Drew Hohn

Despite the assumption in our culture that adults are literate, approximately 24 percent of U.S. adults have problems with reading tasks, and approximately one half have significantly limited literacy skills (Kirsch, Jungeblut, Jenkins, and Kolstad, 1993). These low-literate adults are found in all demographic groups; they are however, more likely to be African American, Hispanic, Native American, or whites of low socioeconomic status (Beder, 1991a; Kirsch, Jungeblut, Jenkins, and Kolstad, 1993). The poor and people of color also experience higher rates of infant mortality (U.S. Department of Health and Human Services, Public Health Service, 1991), are at higher risk for chronic diseases ("Prevalence of Selected Risk Factors for Chronic Disease," 1994), and experience shorter life expectancy (U.S. Bureau of the Census, 1993). In addition, they use preventive health services less frequently than members of other groups (Harlan, Bernstein, and Kessler, 1991) and experience a range of barriers to health care (Mokuau and Fong, 1994; Ross-Lee, Kiss, and Weiser, 1994).

A growing body of evidence from both developing and industrialized countries suggests that a lack of reading skills may contribute to poor health status and outcomes (Grosse and Auffrey, 1989; Weiss, Hart, McGee, and D'Estelle, 1992; Tresserras and others, 1992). A broad-ranging review of health and literacy in Canada (Perrin, 1989b) found that persons with low literacy skills are less healthy: they cannot read medication labels and sometimes take medication wrong; they sometimes mix formula incorrectly and improperly feed infants; they cannot read written instructions for follow-up care; they are less likely to have had a Pap smear or a blood pressure check; their jobs tend to be hazardous, and they get hurt on the job more frequently than other

NEW DIRECTIONS FOR ADULT AND CONTINUING EDUCATION, no. 70, Summer 1996 © Jossey-Bass Publishers

employees; they are less likely to have smoke detectors, fire extinguishers, or first-aid kits in their homes; they smoke more than other groups; they drink more coffee, and have poorer nutrition; they exercise less. Furthermore, because they are often low income, they are more likely to live in substandard housing and in unsafe areas. They may also be less healthy because their access to health care may be thwarted by their lack of information about where to go and when to seek help (Doak, Doak, and Root, 1985; Hartley, 1989; Williams and others, 1995). Patients must comprehend signs and locate clinics; understand and comply with written doctor's orders and follow-up appointments; interpret written pamphlets and brochures; and correctly use prescribed treatment modalities, medications, and diets (Doak, Doak, and Root, 1985; Hartley, 1989; Perrin, 1989a). Health care insurance plans are complex and difficult to interpret, and the inability to read and understand them is also a deterrent to care (Shuptrine, cited in Williams and others, 1995; Sissel, 1995a, 1995b; Williams and others, 1995).

Culture of the Health Care Setting

Historically, populations with low income and low literacy skills have had limited access to health care information. Nearly all public health information is printed, written by skilled readers for skilled readers (Doak and Doak, 1987; Breen, 1993; Weiss, Hart, McGee, and D'Estelle, 1992). Moreover, these written materials often assume that readers' worldviews, cultural orientations, and health needs will reflect a white middle-class perspective (Kappel, 1988; Hohn, 1995). Thus, such information is of virtually no use to the 90 million people in the United States with marginal reading skills (Kirsch, Jungeblut, Jenkins, and Kolstad, 1993) or to those whose language or culture contains different concepts about what health is and how it is maintained. For example, only recently has the phenomenon of patient noncompliance has been tied to the cultural knowledge embedded in prescription and other medical information. A qualitative study of prescription packaging language and symbols (Lippin and Fingeret, 1991) found that their embedded meanings are often inconsistent with the cultural understandings of low-literate adults.

Providers are often unaware that written patient information may be inappropriate for a patient's reading level and cultural perspectives. Studies have found most such literature to be written at the 10th- to 13th-grade level (Davis and others, 1994; Jackson and others, 1991), far above the reading levels of many patients. Patients' reading levels in public health clinics are around the 5th-grade level (Davis and others, 1994; Williams and others, 1995; Jackson and others, 1991; Murphy and others, 1993). Indeed, most health professionals are not yet cognizant of the vital link between literacy and health (Jackson and others, 1991; Morgan, 1993; Plimpton and Root, 1994) or of the fact that adults with low literacy skills have common problems and concerns. For several reasons, providers typically assume that their patients have no problem reading: they are unaware of the extent of low literacy among the population, patients often do not request reading assistance, or patients hide their inability to read because it carries a stigma of shame in this culture (Beder, 1991b; Parikh and others, cited in Miles and Davis, 1995). Indeed, Kirsch, Jungeblut, Jenkins, and Kolstad (1993) found that many low-literate adults describe themselves as reading or writing English well or very well, so that a patient's self-reported reading ability may not correspond with his or her actual skills.

Creation of Partnerships

Making a connection between literacy and health is becoming more common. For example, some clinics and hospitals are making efforts to ascertain patients' reading abilities (Davis and others, 1994; Williams and others, 1995), and techniques for creating and testing readable health information are being advocated (Berger, Inkelas, and Myhre, 1994). Physicians and patient educators are being increasingly sensitized to the need to identify and support low-literate patients (Kanonowicz, 1993; Plimpton and Root, 1994). It is being advocated that health clinics make referrals to literacy providers and promote literacy programs to families (Bean, Southworth, Koebler, and Fotta, 1990; Geissler, 1994; Needlman and Zuckerman, 1993).

Clearly, there is a need for health care information that people can understand and act upon regardless of their literacy level, culture, or language. Developing such equal access to information requires collaboration between the health and the literacy education provider communities, and the involvement of the target groups. Together, they can develop and review materials and educational programs and explore new ways to communicate health information. This learning together entails an exploration of diversity and structural equity issues in the health arena if we are to redress the structural inequality of a health education system that frequently does not honor different cultural perspectives on health or differences in language and reading level, a system that often ignores local community and determines health information needs from the top down.

Hence, the importance of literacy providers' taking a leadership role cannot be overlooked. By using health-related materials in their programming, literacy providers can create an informed community of adults who feel empowered to address issues of health and well-being in their own lives and to confront the health care system that ignores their informational needs. Such literacy programs can have a lasting impact, not only on learners' literacy skills but on the current and future health and well-being of the learners, their families, and their communities (Hohn, 1995; Morris, 1994; Rudd and others, 1994).

Adult Education, Popular Education, and Participatory Research

The work of linking health and literacy education finds its base in theories of adult education (Knowles, 1989), popular education (Arnold, Barndt, and

Burke, 1985; Auerbach, 1992; Freire, 1985; Vella, 1994), and participatory research (Fals-Borda and Rahman, 1991; Gaventa, 1980; Hall, 1994; Maquire, 1987; Park, 1992). Despite significant differences, these theories also hold many common assumptions, beliefs, and values, and their principles and practices have great compatibility. All embrace a deep belief in the capacity of humans to reflect, learn, and grow. All promote the idea that people matter more than institutions and that the people most affected by a problem must be involved in solving that problem in a manner that respects their needs, intelligence, and dignity (Hohn, 1995). Popular education and participatory research extend these beliefs in their insistence that social problems have their roots in organizations and systems, not people (Freire, 1985). Making meaning and making change are perceived as involving local experiences and values and an interweaving of relationships, events, and people (Auerbach, 1992).

Paradigm Shift in Health Promotion Practice

Robertson and Minkler (1994) describe a paradigm shift in health promotion theory and practice that provides an additional base for the linking of health and literacy education. This shift is "broadening the definition of health . . . to include the social and economic context within which health, or more precisely, non-health is produced. . . . [It is] going beyond the earlier emphasis on individual lifestyle strategies to achieve health to broader social and political strategies . . . embracing the concept of empowerment—individual and collective—as a key health promotion strategy . . . and advocating the participation of the community in identifying health problems and strategies for addressing those problems" (pp. 295–296).

   This new thinking mirrors the significant attention being paid to understanding, community involvement, and empowerment in worker health and safety education. Many training programs have shifted from a behavioristic approach (teaching workers safe behaviors) to empowerment programs with the broader goal of promoting worker activism for a healthier work environment. There is increasing interest in learning approaches that are participatory, based on life experiences, incorporate dialogue, and examine root causes in the organization and system (Wallerstein, 1992).

Economic and Legal Forces Affecting Health Care

Changes in the health care system are putting more of the onus on patients to employ preventive health behaviors and to self-administer some treatments. Patients are being discharged from hospitals more quickly (Wallace, 1994) and being asked to monitor their own follow-up care (Schneider and others, 1993). Yet because even the most literate of patients may have problems understanding diagnoses and directions, accreditation organizations are holding hospitals accountable for patients' understanding of discharge instructions

(Koska, 1992), and an emphasis on the use of "plain language" is emerging (Koba, 1993).

Health maintenance organizations (HMOs) with Medicaid contracts are increasingly concerned about reaching difficult-to-access and high-risk Medicaid populations with preventive health programs and health services. Some states are spelling out HMOs' responsibilities to the communities they serve. In Massachusetts, fifteen HMOs have voluntarily entered into standards and guidelines that define what HMOs should do to improve the health of communities and to improve access to health care for such underserved populations as the working poor; children in poverty; victims of domestic violence; low- and moderate-income elders; racial, linguistic, and ethnic minorities; and people with physical or cognitive difficulties (Massachusetts Attorney General, 1996). Participating HMOs agree to ensure that linguistic and cultural differences do not present health care barriers.

Collectively, these systemic changes and the economic and legal forces that are driving them constitute an additional imperative for recognizing and acknowledging literacy-health connections and for establishing partnerships to address them.

Promising New Practices and Programs

It is the participatory approach to producing health education materials that is often the first step in linking health care and literacy education (Doak, Doak, and Root, 1985; Rudd and Comings, 1994; Szudy and Arroyo, 1994). Co-development of materials has opened the door for more extensive partnerships in program development.

Massachusetts has been a leader in linking the literacy and health education systems. The work has grown from the passion and commitment of a small group of literacy and health education practitioners who have connected around common concerns for social justice in health and a belief in a participatory approach that leads to both individual and community empowerment.

The Massachusetts Health Team, formed in 1991, became the vehicle wherein literacy and health practitioners could not only talk about what linkages might look like but also try out ideas, materials, and products. The team's mission was embedded in beliefs that health is socially and culturally defined and cannot be separated from a myriad of interconnected issues (economic status, power, economic class, and gender), that health awareness and individual and social change can be influenced by health education, and that low-literate adults should have the opportunity to investigate health issues with others in a supportive and empowering literacy class setting.

Initial implementation was modest. During 1992 and 1993, the focus was on revising fact sheets on breast and cervical cancer for low-literate audiences for the Cancer Information Service and on developing a participatory education kit about HIV/AIDS for the Massachusetts Health Research Institute. As the vision, energy, and membership within the team accelerated, greater connections were made. In 1993, a collaborative effort began with the Massachusetts Public Health Department, the Massachusetts Cancer Information Service, and SABES (System for Adult Basic Education Support) at World Education. For more than forty-five years, World Education has provided education, health, and employment opportunities for the socially and economically disadvantaged—women, youth, ethnic minorities, and the poor. In addition to literacy, World Education programs include small business development, environmental education, and maternal and child health (education and refugee assistance and training). World Education, in partnership with Harvard University, was recently named the national research and development center for improving adult literacy and learning. The goal of the collaboration was to demonstrate the effectiveness of using literacy programs to communicate information about breast and cervical cancer early detection to persons with limited literacy skills.

Project HEAL. The outgrowth of this collaboration was Project HEAL (Health Education and Adult Literacy), begun in 1994 by World Education to develop and introduce health curricula for literacy classrooms. Funded by national cancer organizations and the Centers for Disease Control, the Breast and Cervical Cancer Kit developed by Project HEAL introduces materials focused on early detection and control of breast and cervical cancer. The kit involves using a participatory approach for appropriate, effective, and empowering teaching and learning about these important cancers, within the context of cultural, informational, and emotional issues, and is a model of the way any health issue might be approached.

As the kit training and facilitation guide (Merson, 1995) points out, the approach has multiple benefits. Adult literacy teachers benefit because health issues are important content for the teaching of reading, writing, oral expression, and math. Adult literacy learners benefit because health issues affect their own wellness and illness and that of their loved ones. Health educators benefit because hard-to-reach but high-risk people in low-income, immigrant, and minority populations are reached and, through them, their families, friends, and neighbors. The kit and its guide are now being used in literacy classrooms in fifteen states and are viewed as an important step in encouraging effective, participatory, and empowering health education in the literacy classrooms. The entire HEAL project stands as both a resource and a model for linking health and literacy education.

Health and literacy projects have also been funded in Massachusetts through the state department of education and tobacco tax dollars. These projects have two goals: to introduce health education and particularly tobacco education into adult literacy classrooms and to develop ways for adult learners to have a say in programming. Twenty-eight projects have been funded, each with differing goals and methodologies. The following example illustrates both the power and the dilemmas in linking health and literacy education in a participatory approach.

Project HEAL at Operation Bootstrap. Operation Bootstrap is a community-based organization located in Lynn, Massachusetts, that offers English as a second language and GED programs and general Adult Basic Education. In cooperation with the Lynn Community Health Center, Operation Bootstrap started its own Project HEAL to develop and implement a participatory health education curriculum. The project began in January 1994 with the creation of the Student Action Health Team, initially composed of seven adult learners, a project facilitator, and a health educator. The team members served as pioneers in the field of health education, exploring decision making and trying out and developing materials. The adult learners—Latino, Asian, Slavic, Haitian, and Anglo—represented the diverse linguistic, cultural, and educational backgrounds of Operation Bootstrap's student population. They were recruited from that population by help-wanted posters and were paid $10 an hour for their participation. The project facilitator coordinated the team's activities, and the health educator provided health-related knowledge and served as a liaison to other health professionals. The facilitator and health educator were not teachers, experts, or controllers but resources and facilitators of processes to help the team do its work, a team where everyone shared responsibility.

By examining the personal health beliefs, experiences, and knowledge of Bootstrap's student body and the health needs students expressed, the team determined content areas to concentrate on and the educational methods to use. Together, team members examined and critiqued current printed health information regarding its adequacy for literacy program students (most print material was found wanting), the messages sent by advertising, and the ways in which institutions (especially health care institutions) operate. Team awareness developed about the interplay between individuals, their environments, and the larger community and society. Team members educated themselves about the health issues they decided were important to cover. Activities stemming from the project included surveys about smoking and condom use, HIV/AIDS education, and violence awareness programs, undertaken in cooperation with a local health agency.

Team members talked eloquently about their experiences and learning in journals and in brochures they produced. "You can learn, and teach your friends, your neighbors, and your family about different [health] topics," noted one of them. "Sometimes we compare the treatment of different diseases from different cultures that I have never heard of. This is a good opportunity for us to teach one another" said another. All embraced the team experience as a way of building confidence and language skills, saying, for example: "I am not as timid, shy, as before," and, "I'm very different now because I know myself better. . . . I can think much better. I feel more confident with myself and more confident to work with different people."

This result did not come without some struggle on the part of both students and facilitator. It required commitment to the process and changes in both students and staff. The facilitator's reflection on her experience with the HIV/AIDS survey team, taken from her journal, exemplifies some of these changes: "This was really tough for me. I kept wanting to 'ask questions'—which I now see is what I do when I disagree: I ask a question, hoping to elicit the response I feel is 'more correct' or better. . . . There is something . . . more fundamental in my thinking now about culture, [that it is] inextricably bound up with privilege and boundaries. . . . I have come to hate the word empowerment—[it] implies someone giving someone something, implies a pouring in. What I see and feel and experience here is more like a blooming, coming from the inside."

Within the changes they achieved, the students found their power and their voice, articulating to the outside world what they had learned about themselves, about health, and about the role of culture in health. They also became advocates for health education in literacy programs and made presentations of their ideas, and materials they developed have been used in various health projects across the state.

Impact of Community-Based Approaches

As can be seen here, the experiences of learners and facilitators in literacy-health education partnerships can be both rewarding and challenging. Still, among those implementing these programs, the question of impact on learners' understanding of health issues and subsequent behavior loomed large. In fact, preliminary studies on Project HEAL (Rudd, 1995) and Operation Bootstrap (Whiton, 1995) indicate that such projects result in definite changes in health behavior and attitudes regarding use and dissemination of health information and use of health care.

Project HEAL (Rudd, 1995) affected learners in three key areas: increased health awareness, attitude and behavior change, and a sense of empowerment as users of health information. For example, learners frequently reported changes in dietary habits and increased frequency of administering breast self-exams. They also indicated that the project influenced them to seek out health information more frequently, increased their level of comfort in using medical and anatomical terms, and helped them discuss sensitive issues related to cancer and illness. In addition, the group-learning experience encouraged participants to become change agents in their families and communities, sharing what they knew with others.

The preliminary findings from Project HEAL show that literacy-health linkages can expand health resources in low-literate and low-income communities. Central to such efforts are learners' access to appropriate health information materials and group dialogue that supports exploration of health issues and sensitizes learners to their own value as health informants to others.

The statewide program of which Operation Bootstrap was a part was evaluated through a qualitative study that explored the perspectives of fifty learners in a variety of literacy-health projects. The learners were asked to discuss their experience with the projects, including the acquiring and disseminating of health information and the use of health materials as a means of developing literacy skills. Findings included information on participants' motivation and interest in participation.

First, the learners overwhelmingly noted that the well-being of their families was what motivated them to learn about health issues. Second, all were able to identify and discuss the new areas of health knowledge they gained as a result of the program. The learners also said that because of the support of their fellow learners, they were able to see their health-related behaviors in a more critical light. They began to view their dietary and smoking habits as problematic, and some were able either to make changes in lifestyle or to contemplate, prepare for, or experiment with behavioral change (Prochaska, DiClemente, and Norcross, 1992). Furthermore, almost half said they shared what they learned with others in their communities. The learners also expressed a sense of empowerment around their new acquisition and use of health information and a sense of pride that they could provide such information to others. Learners had expanded vocabulary skills, but otherwise it was not clear whether learners' literacy skills were enhanced by the use of the health-related materials. More research is needed in this area and in determining how much of a role the participatory classroom approach played in project success.

Directions for the Future

Although various forms of literacy-health partnerships are being reported in the literature, linkages between health care providers, adult educators, and literacy providers are currently not the norm. We will encourage a community-based focus on literacy and health by moving in the following directions in the future:

Further develop and assess health education materials appropriate for low literates. This is imperative.
Increase emphasis on referral and program linkages between health care providers and literacy programs.
Disseminate collaborative program models that inform both fields.
Increase awareness of issues of literacy and health for practitioners in both fields.

As in all new ventures, a myriad of questions and challenges are emerging as the work progresses. Important questions still to be answering include the following:

What is the best way to forge more collaborations between health educators, health care systems, and literacy programs?
How can we ensure that collaborations include learning by *both* low-literate learners and health practitioners?
In what ways can literacy providers promote change in health care provision to ensure that the focus is on changing the system, not blaming the victim?

What are the dangers of incorporating health education in literacy programs? What should the role of the teacher/tutor be? What does it mean in terms of staff development if literacy teachers act as health educators?

In what ways do literacy teachers change by being involved in both health and literacy work? What are the personal and professional enhancements and challenges?

How do we all deal with the personal pain that frequently accompanies health stories and health discussions?

What kinds of evidence will document changes in health knowledge, beliefs, attitudes, and ultimately behavior in a manner that satisfies both health and literacy providers and funders?

Conclusion

Through the development of partnerships between literacy programs and health educators and providers, vital information about health and health resources can be offered to low-literate adults in ways previously unavailable. A community-based approach to literacy and health programming that is participatory and collective results in benefits to all involved: low-literate adults, health and literacy educators, and the health providers who are working to meet the needs of this population.

References

Arnold, R., Barndt, D., and Burke, B. *A New Weave: Popular Education in Canada and Central America.* Toronto: CUSO Development Education and Ontario Institute for Studies in Education—Adult Education Department, 1985.

Auerbach, E. *Making Meaning, Making Change: Participatory Curriculum Development for Adult ESL Literacy.* Washington, D.C.: Center for Applied Linguistics, 1992.

Bean, R. M., Southworth, H., Koebler, S., and Fotta, B. *The Beginning with Books Gift Book Program: Effects on Family and Child Literacy. Final Report.* Pittsburgh, Penn.: University of Pittsburgh, Institute for Practice and Research in Education, 1990.

Beder, H. *Adult Literacy: Issues for Policy and Practice.* Malabar, Fla.: Krieger, 1991a.

Beder, H. "The Stigma of Illiteracy." *Adult Basic Education,* 1991b, 1 (2), 67–78.

Berger, D., Inkelas, M., and Myhre, S. "Developing Health Education Materials for Inner-City, Low Literacy Parents." *Public Health Reports,* 1994, 109, 168–172.

Breen, M. J. *Partners in Practice: The Literacy and Health Project, Phase Two, August 1990–October 1992.* Toronto: Ontario Public Health Association, 1993.

Davis, T. C., Mayeaux, E. J., Fredrickson, D., Bocchini, J. A., Jackson, R., and Murphy, P. W. "Reading Ability of Parents Compared with Reading Level of Pediatric Patient Education Materials." *Pediatrics,* 1994, 93 (3), 460–468.

Doak, L. G., and Doak, C. C. "Lowering the Silent Barriers to Compliance for Patients with Low Literacy Skills." *Health Promotion,* 1987, 8 (4), 6–8.

Doak, L. G., Doak, C. C., and Root, J. *Teaching Patients with Low Literacy Skills.* Philadelphia: Lippincott, 1985.

Fals-Borda, O., and Rahman, M. A. *Action and Knowledge: Breaking the Monopoly with Participatory Action Research.* New York: Apex Press, 1991.

Freire, P. *The Politics of Education: Culture, Power and Liberation.* New York: Bergin & Garvey, 1985.

Gaventa, J. *Power and Powerlessness: Quiescence and Rebellion in an Appalachian Valley*. Champaign: University of Illinois Press, 1980.

Geissler, B. "Literacy-Health Partnerships That Work." *Adult Learning*, 1994, 5 (6), 21–22, 26.

Grosse, R. N., and Auffrey, C. "Literacy and Health Status in Developing Countries." *Annual Review of Public Health*, 1989, 10, 281–297.

Hall, B. "Introduction." In P. Park, M. Byron-Miller, B. Hall, and T. Jackson (eds.), *Voices of Change: Participatory Research in the United States and Canada*. Westport, Conn.: Bergin & Garvey, 1994.

Harlan, L. C., Bernstein, A. B., and Kessler, L. G. "Cervical Cancer Screening: Who Is Not Screened and Why?" *American Journal of Public Health*, 1991, 81, 885–890.

Hartley, R. *The Social Costs of Inadequate Literacy: A Report for International Literacy Year*. Melbourne: Australian Institute of Family Studies, 1989.

Hohn, M. "Linking Health and Literacy Education." Paper presented at the Commission of Adult Basic Education conference, Little Rock, Ark., June 1995.

Jackson, R. H., Davis, T. C., Bairnsfather, L. E., George, R. B., Crouch, M. A., and Gault, H. "Patient Reading Ability: An Overlooked Problem in Health Care." *Southern Medical Journal*, 1991, 84 (10), 1172–1175.

Kanonowicz, L. "National Project to Publicize Link Between Literacy, Health." *Canadian Medical Association Journal*, 1993, 148 (7), 1201–1202.

Kappel, B. "Literacy and Health." *Ontario Medical Review*, 1988, 55 (3), 42–43.

Kirsch, I. S., Jungeblut, A., Jenkins, L., and Kolstad, A. *Adult Literacy in America: A First Look at the Results of the National Adult Literacy Survey (NALS)*. Washington, D.C.: National Center for Education Statistics, U.S. Department of Education, 1993.

Knowles, M. S. *The Making of an Adult Educator: An Autobiographical Journey*. San Francisco: Jossey-Bass, 1989.

Koba, H. "Putting It Plainly Becomes Communication Mission of Ontario's Ministry of Health." *Canadian Medical Association Journal*, 1993, 148 (7), 1202–1203.

Koska, M. T. "JCAHO Introduces Three New Areas of Survey Concentration." *Hospitals*, 1992, 66 (19), 62, 64, 66.

Lippin, T. M., and Fingeret, H. A. *How Adults with Limited Literacy Skills Cope with Reading Medication Labels*. Durham, N.C.: Literacy South, 1991.

Maquire, P. *Doing Participatory Research: A Feminist Approach*. Amherst: Center for International Education, University of Massachusetts, 1987.

Massachusetts Attorney General. *Community Benefit Guidelines for Health Maintenance Organizations*. Boston: Massachusetts Attorney General's Office, 1996.

Merson, M. M. *Project HEAL Facilitator's Guide* (draft version). Boston: World Education, 1995.

Miles, S., and Davis, T. "Patients Who Can't Read: Implications for the Health Care System." *Journal of the American Medical Association*, 1995, 274 (21), 1719–1720.

Mokuau, N., and Fong, R. "Assessing the Responsiveness of Health Services to Ethnic Minorities of Color." *Social Work in Health Care*, 1994, 20 (2), 23–34.

Morgan, P. P. "Illiteracy Can Have Major Impact on Patients' Understanding of Health Care Information." *Canadian Medical Association Journal*, 1993, 148 (7), 1196–1197.

Morris, G. "Integrating Health Education into a Literacy Program." Paper presented at the American Public Health Association conference, Washington, D.C., Nov. 1994.

Murphy, P. W., Davis, T. C., Long, S. W., Jackson, R. H., and Decker, B. C. "Rapid Estimate of Adult Literacy in Medicine (REALM): A Quick Reading Test for Patients." *Journal of Reading*, 1993, 37 (2), 124–130.

Needlman, R., and Zuckerman, B. "Pediatric Interventions to Promote Picture Book Use." Paper presented at the biennial meeting of the Society for Research in Child Development, New Orleans, Mar. 1993.

Park, P. "The Discovery of Participatory Research as a New Scientific Paradigm: Personal and Intellectual Accounts." *American Sociologist*, 1992, 23 (4), 29–42.

Perrin, B. "Literacy and Health: Making the Connection." *Health Promotion*, 1989a, *28* (1), 2–5.

Perrin, B. *Literacy and Health Project. Phase One. Making the World Healthier and Safer for People Who Can't Read.* Toronto: Ontario Public Health Association, 1989b.

Plimpton, S., and Root, J. "Materials and Strategies That Work in Low Literacy Health Communication." *Public Health Reports,* 1994, *109* (1), 86–92.

"Prevalence of Selected Risk Factors for Chronic Disease by Education Level in Racial/ Ethnic Populations—United States, 1991–1992." *Morbidity and Mortality Weekly Report,* 1994, *43* (48), 894–899.

Prochaska, J., DiClemente, C., and Norcross, J. "In Search of How People Change: Applications to Addictive Behavior." *American Psychologist,* Sept. 1992, 1102–1114.

Robertson, A., and Minkler, M. "New Health Promotion Movement: A Critical Examination." *Health Education Quarterly,* 1994, *21* (3), 295–312.

Ross-Lee, B., Kiss, L. E., and Weiser, M. A. "Should Healthcare Reform Be 'Color-Blind?' Addressing the Barriers to Improving Minority Health." *Journal of the American Osteopathic Association,* 1994, *94* (8), 664–671.

Rudd, R. E. "An Exploratory Study: Effects of HEAL Participation." Boston: Harvard School of Public Health, June 1995.

Rudd, R. E., and Comings, J. P. "Learner Developed Materials: An Empowering Product." *Health Education Quarterly,* 1994, *21* (3), 313–327.

Rudd, R. E., McGrail, M. A., Waldron, S., Owen, M., Molnar, C., and Langford, L. "Introducing Health Topics into Literacy Programs." Paper presented at the American Public Health Association conference, Washington, D.C., Nov. 1994.

Schneider, J. K., Hornberger, S., Booker, J., Davis, A., and Kralicek, R. "A Medication Discharge Planning Program: Measuring the Effect on Readmissions." *Clinical Nursing Research,* 1993, 2 (1), 41–53.

Sissel, P. A. *Falling Through the Cracks: An Ethnographic Study of the Get Smart Delta Health Insurance Program.* Little Rock: Center for Applied Research and Evaluation, Department of Pediatrics, University of Arkansas for Medical Sciences, 1995a.

Sissel, P. A. "Literacy and Health: Are We Overlooking the Link?" Paper presented at the 1995 Commission on Adult Basic Education conference, Little Rock, Ark., June 1995b.

Szudy, E., and Arroyo, M. G. *The Right to Understand: Linking Literacy to Health and Safety Training.* Berkeley: Labor Occupation Health Program, University of California, 1994.

Tresserras, R., Canela, J., Alvarez, J., Sentis, J., and Salleras, L. "Infant Mortality, Per Capita Income, and Adult Illiteracy: An Ecological Approach." *American Journal of Public Health,* 1992, *82* (3), 435–438.

U.S. Bureau of the Census. *Statistical Abstract of the United States: 1993.* Washington, D.C.: U.S. Government Printing Office, 1993.

U.S. Department of Health and Human Services, Public Health Service. *Healthy People 2000: National Health Promotion and Disease Prevention Objectives.* Washington, D.C.: U.S. Department of Health and Human Services, 1991.

Vella, J. *Learning to Listen, Learning to Teach: The Power of Dialogue in Educating Adults.* San Francisco: Jossey-Bass, 1994.

Wallace, P. E., Jr. "Post-Hospital Care for the Underserved: A Review." *Journal of Health Care for the Poor and Underserved,* 1994, *5* (4), 316–325.

Wallerstein, N. "Health and Safety Education for Workers with Low-Literacy or Limited-English Skills." *American Journal of Industrial Medicine,* 1992, *22,* 751–765.

Weiss, B. D., Hart, G., McGee, D. L., and D'Estelle, S. "Health Status of Illiterate Adults: Relation Between Literacy and Health Status Among Persons with Low Literacy Skills." *Journal of the American Board of Family Practice,* 1992, *5* (3), 257–264.

Whiton, L. *Ask the Learner: How Does Health Education Impact the Lives of Adult Education Learners?* Boston: Comprehensive Health Education Projects, 1995.

Williams, M. V., Parker, R., Baker, D., Parikh, N., Pitkin, K., Coates, W., and Nurss, J. "Inadequate Functional Health Literacy Among Patients at Two Public Hospitals." *Journal of the American Medical Association,* 1995, 274 (21), 1677–1682.

PEGGY A. SISSEL *is assistant professor, Center for Research on Teaching and Learning, College of Education, University of Arkansas at Little Rock, and adjunct assistant professor, Department of Pediatrics, University of Arkansas for Medical Sciences.*

MARCIA DREW HOHN *is director of SABES (System for Adult Basic Education Support) at North Essex Community College in Lawrence, Massachusetts, and a doctoral student in adult and continuing education at the Fielding Institute.*

Advice for establishing popular education programs, an adult education strategy particularly relevant to community-based organizations, rests on an understanding of the components of popular education and how they function.

Popular Education: An Appropriate Educational Strategy for Community-Based Organizations

Hal Beder

To a great extent, familiarity with popular education in the United States is a product of the popularity of Paulo Freire's writings, particularly *Pedagogy of the Oppressed* (1970). In fact, in the United States, *popular education* is sometimes termed *Freireian education*. Freire is a Brazilian adult educator whose educational philosophy and pedagogy emerged from a Latin American context that views society as bifurcated into an elite class that owns the preponderance of resources and holds all the power and an "oppressed" class that owns little and is powerless. Freire's pedagogy is directed toward creating a nonviolent revolution through adult education. At its most basic level, it focuses on a process of conscientization through which the oppressed come to understand the cultural forces that produce and maintain oppression. Empowered by this new understanding, the oppressed then undertake collective action designed to redress social and material inequality.

When I first read *Pedagogy of the Oppressed* in the early 1970s, I was greatly impressed. On the second and third readings, however, many questions arose, although my enthusiasm for Freire's basic message was not diminished. When and how were the material consequences of oppression, such as endemic hunger and ill health, to be resolved? Although conscientization may be necessary for social change, was it alone sufficient? While I understood what popular educators believed in, what did popular educators actually do? In short, like so many of my contemporaries, I had embraced the theory of popular education, but I was bewildered by the practice of it.

I have since learned that the roots of popular education considerably predate Freire and that a sophisticated and systematic methodology of popular

NEW DIRECTIONS FOR ADULT AND CONTINUING EDUCATION, no. 70, Summer 1996 © Jossey-Bass Publishers

education practice has developed in Latin America. When I studied popular education in Mexico, Peru, and Chile (supported by, among others, CEAAL [Consejo de Educacíon de Adultos de América Latina], a coordinating network of popular educators that operates throughout Latin America), my appreciation and understanding of popular education expanded, and I began to reflect more and more on how the Latin American experience might be adapted to the U.S. context. In 1991, following an educational exchange program involving the International Council for Adult Education and FLASEP (Fundacíon Latinoamericana de Apoyo al Saber y la Economia Popular), a Mexican popular education nongovernmental organization, the Participatory Adult Education Group (PAEG) developed. PAEG has charged itself with the ongoing adaptation of Latin American popular education methods to its members' practice and with disseminating what has been learned to others.

In both Latin America and the United States, popular education is most commonly practiced by community-based organizations (CBOs) rather than governmental agencies. There are at least two reasons for this. First, the bottom-up grassroots orientation of popular education is compatible with the ways CBOs typically operate and antithetical to the bureaucratic top-down operation of governmental agencies. Second, and perhaps more important, popular education is compatible with the ideological orientation of CBOs that work with marginalized people to effect significant societal change and to promote social justice, an ideology aptly expressed in this definition of popular education: "education that serves the interests of the popular classes (exploited sectors of society), that involves them in critically analyzing their social situation and in organizing to act collectively to change the oppressive conditions of their lives" (Arnold, Barndt, and Burke, 1985, p. 5).

Depending on the context in which it is practiced, such popular education takes many forms. Indeed forms of it were practiced in some U.S. organizations long before the term popular education was known here (the Highlander Center in New Market, Tennessee, is an excellent example). However, because so much popular education theory derives from Latin America and my own orientation has been influenced by my Latin American experience, I focus on a Latin American perspective in this chapter. The chapter defines popular education both conceptually and descriptively, discusses beginning a popular education program, and concludes with a list of resources.

What Is Popular Education?

In nearly every popular education training session I have attended, the question of what popular education is has been central, particularly in discussions about goals. Although there is agreement on the basic components of popular education, different organizations emphasize different components. Advocacy-based CBOs, for example, typically emphasize collective action directed toward social change, and education-oriented agencies tend to emphasize educational components. This diversity underscores the flexibility of the popular education model. However, most popular educators would agree that popular education has three essential and integrated components that separate it from other adult education methodologies: praxis, a collective and participatory orientation, and action.

Praxis. If a desire to change society for the better is the heart of popular education, praxis is its brain. Praxis is the interaction between theory and practice, in which theory informs practice and practice informs theory. Collective critical reflection is the process that creates the interaction. The product of praxis is new knowledge that is specific to a given context or problem and that informs collective action. Praxis is an ongoing process that pervades all aspects of popular education decision making. After an action is taken, for example, results are analyzed through collective critical reflection, and the theory that guided the action is modified accordingly. For praxis to be effective, all three components—theory, collective critical reflection, and practice—must be present. Praxis is at the heart of the problem-posing method in popular education. An example from Mexico demonstrates how this method works.

Mexico City, the world's largest city, represents an enormous market for dairy products, yet the small dairy farmers who ringed the city could barely make ends meet. A peasants' union brought its members together to address this problem in a meeting facilitated by a popular educator. The first stage was to specify the problem to be resolved, and consensus was reached easily: "Our income from dairy production is so low that we cannot feed our families." The second stage was to identify the social, economic, and historical forces that had produced the problem. Through collective critical reflection facilitated by the popular educator, the dairymen developed an initial theory: their production costs were so high that the price of their milk was continually undercut by more efficient large-scale producers. They had no access to the large market in the city. The quality of their livestock was poor, and milk output per cow was low. This theory, though basic, represented the first step in the praxis model.

The group members then decided that they needed more information to refine the basic theory and to inform potential collective action. For example, they analyzed feed prices and learned that large-scale producers paid less by purchasing in quantity. They also learned that most milk consumed in the city was reconstituted dry milk, because that was all that was available. Thus, there was a large potential market for their whole milk product if they could pasteurize it and get it to market before it soured. The farmers were now to begin the step of action. A purchasing collective was established that resulted in lower feed prices and lower milk production costs, and a milk cooperative was established to develop producer-owned pasteurizing, bottling, and market transportation plants.

Although theory generated through collective critical reflection on experience and systematically collected information resulted in this action, the praxis process has not stopped. The buildings and equipment acquired for the milk production plants are still not in operation due to the lack of initial operating capital. Therefore, a new cycle of praxis was initiated to determine how to acquire that capital. Through critical reflection on their experience in establishing the collective, the peasants created new knowledge and expanded their initial theory. This knowledge is now being used to establish producer-owned dry goods and food stores that sell at lower prices to members and produce profits to be invested elsewhere.

Collective and Participatory Orientation. In contrast to most adult education methodologies practiced in the United States, popular education is a collective methodology, in all aspects. Groups rather than individuals are the object of education, the process is highly participatory, and although individuals may benefit, program outcomes are measured by group achievements.

Groups as the Object of Education. Popular education typically begins with a group of adults who have a shared need to solve a problem or problems. In some cases, the group disbands once the problem has been solved, but more often the group stays intact through multiple cycles of problem solving. One of the more perplexing problems that faces popular educators, particularly in the United States, is how to create popular education groups when individuals lack awareness of their common problems or when they are so alienated and disempowered that they do not believe group action can make a difference.

Group Process. Popular education is conducted by, with, and for the participants. For popular education to *be* popular education, authority for all aspects of decision making, including resource allocation, must rest clearly with group members. It could be no other way in a form of education that is vitally concerned with democracy and an end to oppressive relationships. There are also pragmatic reasons that clients or members must "own" the popular education process. If lasting change is to be created, a lasting infrastructure for collective social action must be developed, including participatory leadership, ability to work in teams, communication structures, and the like. Infrastructures based on dependency relationships are seldom lasting—when the external leader or patron leaves, the infrastructure all too often collapses. Capacitation is a major goal of popular education, and true capacitation cannot be achieved unless power is vested with the participants.

It is also true that an educational process based on collective learning and group process greatly expands the potential for learning. In the traditional model, the knowledge a teacher conveys to an individual is the only knowledge brought to bear. In the collective model, however, the knowledge and experience of the entire group can be used. Moreover, through a division of labor in which individuals and teams amass and then share knowledge about a specific issue, the total amount of useful knowledge available for problem solving is greatly increased.

As has been said, praxis requires collective learning because it depends on collective critical reflection. Through the collective critical reflection process, information and theory are transformed into operational theory, which then informs practice and action. Because popular education is collective, many of its techniques are designed to manage and promote the success of group process. Positive group dynamics are not considered an end in themselves or a means to individual therapy, however. Rather, successful group process is a means to further learning and successful collective action.

The experience of the Participatory Adult Education Group (PAEG) exemplifies popular education's collective orientation (Participatory Adult Education Group, 1993). PAEG supports popular education through staff development, functioning as a laboratory that experiments with popular education methods and techniques and refines them through collective critical reflection. Through such reflection on its experience with Mexican popular education, PAEG identified four functions vital to its success: coordination, communication, community, and systematization. Communication and community were directly related to participation and a collective orientation. Communication was considered both vital and problematic: collective planning and reflection required effective communication because group members seldom were able to meet face-to-face. Community was considered vital because the group could not work collectively unless all its members were included in decisions and had equal voices.

After considering several mechanisms to ensure communication and community, PAEG established "commissions" to oversee these functions. These commissions are central parts of the permanent organizational structure, and temporary community and communication commissions are established for meetings and activities. The communications commission is charged with establishing effective communication with all members and monitoring the effectiveness of communication at all events. When problems in communication are identified, they are reported to the whole group for collective reflection and problem solving. Because the membership is geographically disbursed, e-mail and faxes are used extensively, and the group is organizing a listserve and Internet homepage. Similarly, the community commission is charged with maintaining community among the membership and monitoring the extent to which all members are included in decision-making and learning activities. When community breaks down, the community commission identifies the problem and resolves it if it can. If it cannot, the problem is reported to the whole group for problem resolution.

Action. Although critical theory, postmodern analysis, feminist research, and certain forms of therapy all employ critical reflection, popular education differs in that the critical reflection goal is always some sort of concrete action, for as Freire (1970) states, reflection without action degenerates into unproductive verbalism while action without reflection "negates the true praxis and makes dialogue impossible" (p. 76). Moreover, the kind of action taken is important. It is conceivable that the basic methods of popular education could be used for evil ends: for example, to further the goals of a white supremacist movement. Therefore, action must further humanist goals such as social justice, social equality, and the elimination of social oppression.

Although praxis, a collective and participatory orientation, and action are key popular education components, they are often difficult to achieve in practice. CBOs faced with enormous tasks and lean resources have difficulty finding the time for collective critical reflection. Use of overworked volunteer staff makes it difficult to include everyone in participatory decision making. A crisis orientation often makes reflective action problematic. The organizational culture of popular education is frequently alien to other organizations popular education programs must work with. Yet despite these constraining factors, it is important that the core components of popular education be maintained. When they are not, popular education organizations transform themselves into traditional social organizations, losing the benefits of popular education.

Additional Important Components. In addition to praxis, a collective orientation, and action, three other components are important to popular education's success: systematization, communication, and attention to the material, or "daily," needs of participants. Systematization is the management of popular education, the component that "rationalizes" the popular education process (Cadena, 1991). If praxis is to be successful, collective critical reflection must be based on reality because critical reflection on false knowledge obviously leads to inappropriate action. But in a praxis-based system, how do participants know what is real and what is not? There are two interconnected answers. First, in popular education, reality and truth are not givens. Rather, reality and truth must be discovered through dialogue and critical analysis. For this reason, the issue of what is real and true must always be a topic of ongoing critical reflection. Second, the object of reflection must be solid and accurate information, and that is precisely what systematization is designed to provide. Through systematization—including maintaining and analyzing documents and records, action research, and ongoing evaluation, both formal and informal—experience is carefully documented, both in process and at the end of a decision-making cycle. Documentation results then become the foundation for collective critical reflection resulting in new action.

Authentic and meaningful communication among popular education participants is also vital if the program is to be truly democratic and participatory and if the collective critical reflection and dialogue necessary for praxis are to be conducted successfully. In communities and groups where members interact constantly face-to-face, communication is essentially a process issue, and there are many techniques in the popular education repertoire designed to enhance it. When participants cannot interact regularly face-to-face, communication becomes a structural challenge as well, and effective systems to promote it must be designed and implemented.

Like participants in any form of voluntary adult education, participants in popular education believe that participation will benefit them. Although the intrinsic benefits that derive from community, dignity, and empowerment are important in popular education, meeting participants' basic material needs through popular education is also important. Central in Latin American forms of popular education, this point receives much less emphasis from Freire. However, as Bunch (1982) notes, a discussion of material needs must be a focus in problem identification, and initial and visible success at meeting basic material needs builds infrastructure by enhancing participants' motivation to tackle more complex and difficult problems.

Outcomes of Popular Education. CBOs that embrace popular education usually do so because they believe it effective for producing outcomes to which they are both philosophically and pragmatically committed—including empowerment, capacitation, and sustainable social change. Although individuals often do become empowered, the important outcome is collective—the empowerment of a group to transform a social situation. Collective empowerment is produced in two ways. First, as Freire notes, groups are disempowered through cultural mechanisms that control them because they are not aware of them. When marginalized groups become conscientized—when they understand the social, political, and economic forces producing their marginalization—they are then able to overcome these forces, and in the process, become empowered. Second, and equally important, when groups solve the needs confronting them and improve their material well-being, success itself breeds collective empowerment.

Capacitation is another outcome of popular education: groups develop leadership and communication systems and learn how to deal with conflict resolution, democratic decision making, strategic planning, and the like. This knowledge, gained through praxis, constitutes an infrastructure, which capacitates the group for successful future action. Collective empowerment and capacitation together create sustainable development and change, development that lasts instead of development that evaporates as soon as funding is retracted and professional staff leave.

How to Do It

Doing popular education begins with a commitment to the basic principles of popular education. The commitment is probably genuine if your organization can answer yes to each of the following questions: Will all members of your group or organization have a meaningful voice in the important decisions? Will information about finances, grant acquisition, and personnel actions be freely available to all organization members? Will collective critical reflection be the ongoing process through which decisions are made and action is planned? Are you more concerned with the collective success of group members than you are with their success as individuals? Are you committed to humanistic social change?

When the commitment is genuine, the details tend to fall into place. This is true because popular education is not only a system for goal attainment but also a system of knowledge production—programs learn how to do popular education by doing it. That is the beauty of praxis.

The process of popular education is typically initiated by a facilitator who assists with problem identification and the establishment of the praxis system. Facilitation is a technical function that requires skills in group process and knowledge of popular education technique. When several people in an organization possess these skills and knowledge, the role of facilitator often rotates. When no one possesses these skills, an outside consultant is often brought in until the capacity for facilitation is established within the organization. As the process of popular education proceeds, a leadership infrastructure and division of labor develop. At this stage, power becomes an issue. Power is a critical resource in popular education, because change cannot be accomplished without power. However, power must be owned by the group, not by individuals, and individuals must exercise power on behalf of the group, not for self-serving reasons. To ensure that power is power-with, not power-over, power relationships should be an ongoing topic of collective critical reflection.

Praxis is a context specific system where one size never fits all. Knowledge of how to do practice in a given context is generated through praxis, and for this reason, popular education programs differ widely in how they configure specifics. Although what is learned in one program context almost always has to be adapted to another, the process of adaptation is an important component of praxis. For this reason, it is very useful for popular education programs to form networks so that they can learn from and support each other.

When CBOs establish popular education programs, one question that often surfaces is, "How do we know that we are doing it right?" Popular education is based on a set of ideals, not a set of rules, not an orthodoxy. If, on critical reflection, a popular education program is confident that it has adhered to the basic principles of popular education, and if its practice is meeting with success as defined by the program, then it is being done correctly. The relevant question for reflection then becomes, "Can it be done better?"

Challenges

A series of challenges often confront CBOs using a popular education methodology. Left unmet, they can threaten the popular education orientation. Some examples:

The grants and funding sources for our program demand that we meet certain objectives. Furthermore, authority for decision making is vested in our board of directors. We need to find a way to engage in collective decision making and still meet the demands of our funding source and articles of incorporation.

We need to meet the needs of, and be accountable to, our members and still meet the accountability requirements of our funding source.

We are so busy reacting to crises and the daily demands of our work that we have no time for collective critical reflection.

We want to do popular education, but our superiors refuse to relinquish the power they hold over us by virtue of their position in the hierarchy.

Our traditional funding sources and the other organizations we work with

think popular education is too radical and revolutionary. If we embrace popular education, they will shut us out and cut us off.
The population we work with is alienated, powerless, and used to a handout. Organizing these individuals for praxis and collective action seems impossible.

Such challenges will have to be resolved through their praxis. There are no easy or off-the-shelf answers.

Resources

The following list of basic resources may be helpful to North American CBOs considering a popular education program.

The Highlander Center. The Highlander Center has an important place in U.S. twentieth-century social history and may well be the best-known and most venerable popular education and training center in this country. Founded by Myles Horton, Highlander has an expert staff, and a comprehensive library of relevant materials. It publishes a selective bibliography and sells a number of salient publications at reasonable prices. Visitors are welcome. Contact: Highlander Research and Education Center, 1959 Highlander Way, New Market, TN 37820–9233.

Doris Marshall Institute. The Doris Marshall Institute is a popular education consulting and support group located in Toronto, Canada. It distributes a number of very practical publications on popular education practice, techniques, and exercises, including the following notable items:

Arnold, R., Barndt, D., and Burke, B. *A New Weave: Popular Education in Canada and Central America.* Toronto: CUSO Development Education and Ontario Institute for Studies in Education—Adult Education Department, 1985.

Arnold, R., and Burke, B. *A Popular Education Handbook: An Educational Experience Taken from Central America and Adapted to the Canadian Context.* Toronto: CUSO Development Education and Ontario Institute for Studies in Education—Adult Education Department, 1985.

Arnold, R., and others. *Educating for a Change.* Toronto: Doris Marshall Institute for Education and Action, 1991.

Barndt, D. *Naming the Moment: Political Analysis for Action.* Toronto: Jesuit Center for Social Faith and Justice, 1989.

Marshall, J. *Training for Empowerment: A Kit of Materials for Popular Literacy Workers Based on an Exchange Among Educators from Mozambique, Nicaragua and Brazil.* Toronto: International Council for Adult Education, n.d.

Contact: Doris Marshall Institute for Education and Action, 25 Cecil St., 2nd floor, Toronto, Ontario M5T 1N1, Canada; telephone (416) 593–8863, fax (416) 593–5267.

North American Alliance for Popular and Adult Education (NAAPAE). NAAPAE is an association of popular educators established to advance the popular and adult education movement in North America, share and advance critical analysis of practice, speak for the North American popular education movement in the international community, and develop links with other regions of the world (North American Alliance for Popular and Adult Education, 1994). Membership is open to any popular education organization that agrees with NAAPAE's mission and goals. Contact: NAAPAE, Box 9, Station P, Toronto, Ontario M5S 2J0, Canada.

Adult Literacy. Adult literacy programs are receiving considerable attention from popular educators. From the popular education perspective, literacy is a means to conscientization and social change rather than an end in itself. As Freire and Macedo (1987, p. 159) explain, "a person is literate to the extent that he or she is able to use the language for social and political reconstruction." SABES (System for Adult Basic Education Support) (also mentioned in Chapter Six) is an adult literacy education staff development system that employs many popular education concepts and methods in its work. Funded by the state of Massachusetts and coordinated by World Education, Inc., SABES has organized workgroups of teachers who use a praxis-based methodology to identify problems from their practice, to generate the knowledge needed to solve them, and to act. Contact: SABES, World Education, Inc., 44 Farnsworth St., Boston, MA 02210.

Conclusion

Popular education is an appropriate strategy for many CBOs that serve marginalized populations because it is compatible with grassroots organization, it seeks to achieve social justice, and is targeted at sustainable development. Praxis, a collective orientation, and action are critical components of popular education. For popular education to be successful, CBOs must be committed to its goals and philosophy and must implement its critical components.

References

Arnold, R., Barndt, D., and Burke, B. *A New Weave: Popular Education in Canada and Central America.* Toronto: CUSO Development Education and Ontario Institute for Studies in Education—Adult Education Department, 1985.

Bunch, R. *Two Ears of Corn: A Guide to People-Centered Agricultural Development.* Oklahoma City, Okla.: World Neighbors, 1982.

Cadena, F. "Transformation Through Knowledge—Knowledge Through Transformation." *Convergence,* 1991, 24 (3), 62–70.

Freire, P. *Pedagogy of the Oppressed.* New York: Seabury Press, 1970.

Freire, P., and Macedo, D. *Literacy: Reading the Word and the World.* New York: Bergin & Garvey, 1987.

North American Alliance for Popular and Adult Education. *NAAPAE, a Movement North.* Toronto: North American Alliance for Popular and Adult Education, 1994.

Participatory Adult Education Group. *The Participatory Adult Education Group: Operational Plan.* New Brunswick, N.J.: Participatory Adult Education Group, 1993.

HAL BEDER is professor of adult and continuing education, Graduate School of Education, Rutgers, the State University of New Jersey.

A staff development process can be based on reflection within the context of a learning community.

"A Wonderfully Terrible Place to Be": Learning in Practitioner Inquiry Communities

Susan L. Lytle

Historically, professional and staff development in adult literacy education either has been narrowly focused on training for using specific materials or tests or has consisted of one-shot workshops on a range of disparate topics. Typically, these encounters make little effort to address the larger questions—pedagogical, political, social and cultural—that inform practitioners' daily work or to assist practitioners to explore what they think is interesting and challenging in their own classrooms. Furthermore, much professional development is seen as remedial, meant to fill identified gaps in knowledge and designed around the knowledge transmission or banking model, in which experts deposit information in the minds of practitioners.

More recently, however, alternative perspectives on staff development in the field of adult literacy have begun to emerge. Rather than focusing on altering people's practices, beliefs, and understandings and on training practitioners by transmitting predetermined skills and knowledge, these new perspectives

This chapter is based in part on the work of the Adult Literacy Practitioner Inquiry Project (ALPIP), funded from 1990 to 1995 by the National Center on Adult Literacy (NCAL) at the University of Pennsylvania. Additional funding for this research came from the Spencer Foundation, and for continuation of the ALPIP local network from the UPS Foundation and the Philadelphia Writing Project. I wish to acknowledge all the participants in ALPIP—especially Richard Drucker, Jean Fleschute, Daryl Gordon, Pat Haff, Sandy Harrill, Peggy McGuire, and Jane McGovern—whose work is quoted here; the research assistance and cofacilitation of Alisa Belzer and Rebecca Reumann on the NCAL ALPIP project; and the many contributions of Elizabeth J. Cantafio to all phases of this chapter.

explicitly position teachers and administrators as active and reflective, as constructors of their own professional practice and generators as well as users of knowledge. In this view, practitioners need opportunities to think deeply about their own work and to reshape work environments for reflective and collaborative dialogue. They also need to be offered support to act on their own conclusions.

Inquiry-based professional development, as I am defining it here, is adult learning that purposefully builds on the richness and diversity of real-world experience and knowledge that teachers, tutors, and administrators possess. It is a systematic and intentional approach involving the collection, analysis, and interpretation of data gathered in classroom and program sites. *Systematic* refers "primarily to ordered ways of gathering and recording information, documenting experiences inside and outside of classrooms, and making some kind of written record. Systematic also refers to ordered ways of recollecting, rethinking, and analyzing classroom events for which there may be only partial or unwritten records." *Intentional* means "that teacher research is an activity that is planned rather than spontaneous." *Inquiry* suggests "that teacher research stems from or generates questions and reflects teachers' desires to make sense of their experiences—to adopt a learning stance or openness toward classroom life" (Cochran-Smith and Lytle, 1993, p. 24).

Practitioner inquiry (or teacher research) may involve close observation, documentation, and analysis of something going on in a tutoring session, classroom, or program, or it may involve some deliberate intervention or change in response to a perceived problem or question. When practitioners come together to conduct inquiries, they raise questions about their assumptions and beliefs, about what counts as learning in their classes, and about the frequent disjunctions in the relationships of programs, families, and communities. Inquiry is not a staff development technique or method. It is a radically different way for practitioners to position themselves as generators, not merely consumers, of significant knowledge for improving practice. They position themselves as learners from what they do every day. A wide range of strategies to initiate and support inquiry are possible, but all involve processes of articulating questions, interacting with colleagues and the literature, closely observing and documenting practice, and possessing an intention to make problematic the social, cultural, cognitive, and political arrangements that structure literacy teaching and learning in particular contexts and communities. Systematic and intentional processes of learning from one's own practice come to be regarded as integral to teaching and administering programs and as critical for making decisions about practice over time.

As a result, practitioners require opportunities to learn that are embedded in their workplace routines and cultures. Teachers and others with whom they work need time and support to invent *local* solutions to their concerns. Classrooms and programs must come to be regarded as inquiry sites and sources of knowledge. This knowledge is most effectively accessed when practitioners come together in groups or communities to examine, and perhaps to alter, their assumptions, beliefs, and daily practices. Taking their classrooms and programs as sites of inquiry into learning, teaching, and assessing, practitioners articulate and question their own interpretive frameworks and theories for understanding practice.

This approach to professional and staff development intentionally blurs the lines between teaching and inquiry and between research and practice. Teachers, tutors, and administrators, together with adult learners, come to play a central role in deciding what counts as knowledge, who can have knowledge, and how knowledge can be generated, challenged, and evaluated.

In this way, systematic inquiry by field-based practitioners becomes a distinctive and important way of knowing about and improving practice. Moreover, the knowledge acquired is both local and public (Lytle and Cochran-Smith, 1993). It is local insofar as practitioners, researching individually and collaboratively, come to understand their own practice. It is public insofar as it informs university-based researchers and teacher educators, policy makers, funders, and government administrators. Finally, by privileging insider questions and knowledge, this approach to professional development allows practitioners to impel their own growth and strengthens the intellectual and social foundations of practice. Indeed, a critical component of this new perspective on professional development is that it brings practitioners—individually and collectively—to the foreground as architects and agents of change.

Building Practitioner Inquiry Communities

In the remainder of this chapter, I describe the work of the Adult Literacy Practitioner Inquiry Project as one example of what it means to build a practitioner inquiry community, and I explore some of the corollaries of working together in inquiry-based development for diverse groups of literacy educators and learners.

Creating the Uncommon Conversation. It is well known that the professional culture often works against practitioners' articulating and raising questions and that practitioners often find themselves quite isolated in their day-to-day work. Practitioner inquiry groups can become vital intellectual communities, providing a rare context for co-laboring around common concerns. There is considerable research to suggest that learning is a deeply social and cultural process, and that the most significant learning occurs when learners are interdependent rather than independent, when their actions and procedures are socially mediated and negotiated. An inquiring community of practitioners, then, becomes more than a context where individual teachers investigate their own topics and the community is much more than a sounding board, more than a provider of support.

The Adult Literacy Practitioner Inquiry Project (ALPIP) is a cross-program, field-university community of practitioner researchers. Begun in 1990 as a research project funded by the National Center on Adult Literacy (NCAL) and the Philadelphia Writing Project, ALPIP has allowed groups of literacy educators—teachers, tutors, and administrators from diverse literacy programs and communities in urban Philadelphia—to come together over the past six years in "seminars" to construct, implement, and at the same time investigate an inquiry-based approach to professional and staff development and knowledge generation for the field.

Although the various ALPIP seminar groups evolve distinctive concerns and processes, they have some common ways of working together that foster a rich and ongoing dialogue. Each group begins with a "common inquiry," a topic chosen by group members as a context and frame for interrogating their literacy histories, day-to-day experiences, and the cultures of the various programs, colleges, and communities in which they do literacy work. The overarching topic is also an organizing device as they mine their diverse responses to writings by other field- and university-based researchers. Using their shared investigations to "stir the pot," group members gradually establish ground rules for working together that explicitly privilege uncertainty and highlight differences and deliberately keep the group or individuals within it from seeking premature closure on sensitive topics. Conversations are premised on the importance of questioning the status quo, on not taking what seems natural as inevitable, on critically examining the antecedents of current practices, and on challenging prevailing explanations (for example, for the lack of equal access to educational opportunities).

Many of the ALPIP groups' conversations have been about the schools' failure to educate culturally diverse populations and about the profound disjunctions that too often exist among learners, families, communities, programs, and schools and school systems and between practitioners and university-based researchers. To discuss these issues openly in diverse groups means investigating the meanings of difference in practitioners' and learners' ethnicities as well as confronting limitations in people's knowledge of values and cultures different from their own. Much attention is paid to learners' stances on learning, their expectations for literacy programs coupled with their schooling histories, the complexities of learners' lives, and differences between and among teachers and learners. A group may begin with a consideration of various definitions of literacy, perspectives on adult learners, and views on the nature of literacy education, including research related to reading, writing, and assessment. Much of the reading comes from practitioner-researchers' writings from all levels of the system. Participants meet in small journal groups to discuss what they have read and written since the last session. They may also meet groups based on job similarity and do a variety of inquiry-based activities to look critically at the readings and their own practice.

An important dimension of the seminars has been the opportunity for participants to meet over time to build relationships and to deepen the possibilities for dialogue. The practitioners have decided that meeting about three hours every other week is a meaningful commitment to working together on critical issues of practice. In addition, participants read and keep journals, conduct classroom and program-based inquiries, and sometimes meet in smaller groups at their worksites.

Around the midpoint of the year, participants create portfolios, identifying recurrent themes in the writing they have done and then imagining the possibilities for closer study over the rest of the year. In these portfolios, participants also reflect generally on connections between the inquiry seminar and their own practice, critique the process of the seminar, and make recommendations. Thus, the portfolio process serves as a review and synthesis of the first phase of the inquiry and as a springboard for more sustained research projects.

The second phase of the professional development seminars continues the discussion of critical issues and begins consideration of practitioner inquiry questions and methods. Recent groups have come to pay considerable attention to understanding and reenvisioning practitioner inquiry to make it congruent with their own knowledge, histories, and current settings. These discussions focus on the ethics of practitioner inquiry; relationships of teachers, administrators, and learners in the research process; and the use of research for various purposes and for local as well as wider audiences. Participants typically form and re-form smaller topic-based research groups and present their data to these subgroups and to the larger group using structured oral inquiry processes.

The seminars typically have practitioner facilitators, sometimes in collaboration with university-based faculty and graduate students who are or who have been literacy practitioners. Group structures require continuous fine-tuning as issues surface about meeting participants' range of needs and expectations. Because the seminars are participatory, tensions may emerge over participant roles, time constraints, responsibilities, and the complexities of planning without precluding spontaneity and invention. Seminars are also appropriately complicated by member diversity of race, class, gender, and program position and by the sometimes competitive environment for literacy programs in the city more generally. These differences are particularly important in considering a group's practices when members share and respond to each other's data. A central task has been developing effective ways to mine possibilities for analysis from members' different frameworks. Participants strive to emphasize the posing and unpacking of problems rather than immediate solutions, and to elaborate rather than narrow their own frameworks for inquiry.

The following section illustrates further the kinds of questions and inquiries these communities support.

Questioning Practices. Practitioners' inquiry projects reveal ways that literacy teachers and administrators attempt to understand their own situations, often in relation to profound tensions and disjunctions in their immediate settings and in relation to the wider field of adult literacy education. Inquiry questions, although in some senses unique to individuals and contexts, also cluster around central themes that cut across the group. For example, in one group, each project included an underlying, if not explicit, concern with understanding, defining, and investigating the nature of literacy and power relationships in classes and programs. These concerns seem to reflect the reality that there are competing paradigms of adult learning and literacy and that the range of program types (often with inconsistent assumptions about literacy learning and the nature of adult learners) sometimes results in uneasy or ill-defined mandates for teacher roles, appropriate curriculum, and classroom formats. Many of the inquiry projects wrestled with the nature of literacy: What should the content of instruction be? How should it be presented? In what ways should learners be involved? What do practitioners need to know to do their job?

The seminar groups' concern with power relationships grew out of shifting and sometimes contradictory images of adult literacy learners as they are portrayed in the popular media and in the research literature (Lytle, 1991). A view of adult learners with multiple literacies that assumes competence and ability raises many questions about the roles that adult learners can and ought to play in planning and implementing instruction. Practitioners encounter tensions, however, as they struggle to answer questions about sharing power, co-creating the curriculum, and putting learners at the center of decision making. Many of the projects dealt explicitly or implicitly with questions of learner-centeredness and power. Practitioners struggled with the contradictions inherent in inviting learners to make decisions to direct their own learning when the learners have not asked for and may not appear to seek this level of control. Many of the projects raised questions about who really makes decisions, under what circumstances, and why. These concerns reflect conflict within the field over whether traditional schooling models and teaching deny access yet again to learners who have not in the past been well "served" by school.

The research questions of practitioners thus reflected dissonances created by complex interactions among a person's professional philosophy and role, the program and seminar contexts, the policy climate in the wider field, and the demands of daily practice. One program administrator, for example, found that her question grew in large measure from pressure from funders and from the gap she perceived between her program's philosophy and its staff development practices. Writing up her inquiry project, she defined her role as being responsible for ensuring that the program is accountable to program participants, funders, and policy makers, not always a simple task. As she explains it, "part of my job is to develop program guidelines which strike a balance between two (sometimes conflicting, and always dynamic) sets of expectations about what constitutes effective adult basic/literacy education practice." This participant's project, which focused on creating a staff development plan for her program, sought to create just such a balance. She asked: "If we are trying to be an authentically community-based, participatory and empowering educational effort in all aspects of [our program], then what constitutes staff development for us, and what is the connection between it and overall organizational development?" (McGuire, 1993, pp. 3–4). Expressing a desire to make the practice of staff development as congruent as possible with program philosophy, she sees a potential gap and chooses, through the implementation of her inquiry project, to work to bridge the distance.

Embedding Research in Practice. To further their own professional development and enhance their practice through the ALPIP community, practitioners selected research methods that were congruent with their day-to-day practice. Inquiry procedures were not simply another set of tasks superimposed on already large workloads but were, helpfully, embedded in the daily work. In one group, practitioners systematically collected various types of information in ways characteristic of qualitative research: document reviews, interviews, and observation with field notes and audio- and videotapes. Document review was used to gather data about such topics as policy, student performance, and student-teacher interactions. Other documents reviewed were created in the classroom or used there, including student writing, a formal reading assessment, and class materials. And sometimes the practitioner-researcher created documents (either alone or with learners), including teacher journals, teacher plans, and teacher-learner dialogue journals. Individual and focus-group interviews produced data on the nature of teaching and learning, based on the perspectives, knowledge, and experiences of others. Teachers and tutors, focusing their observations with their inquiry questions, observed tutoring sessions, writing workshops, reading and discussion of texts, and ongoing teacher-learner interaction. Practitioners documented both their observations and interviews by taking field notes and sometimes using audio- or videotapes.

Practitioners incorporated data collection into their practice in different ways. Sometimes they examined an existing activity more closely, observing learners' responses in a more systematic and intentional way. More often, inquiry projects provided an impetus for practitioners to try something new using existing class or program structures. Thus, the inquiry took place during class or as part of regularly scheduled meetings or events. Another approach to braiding together research and practice involved introducing new formats that were not part of the regular program or class routines, such as focus groups or a dialogue journal between teacher and administrator. These new formats, however, always grew out of existing program issues or staff and learner concerns, thus representing insider perspectives and offering the possibility of providing information or insight needed by program participants.

Generating Local and Public Knowledge. In ALPIP seminar groups, practitioner inquiries addressed interpretative questions that reflected distinctive contexts and spoke to the concerns of multiple audiences in the field. Although practitioner-researchers were obviously their own first audiences, the deeply contextualized questions raised in their research also spoke to the concerns of fellow participants in the local practitioner-research community. Through a year-long process of dialogue and exchange about readings in adult literacy education and related issues in their practice, and through development of research questions and eventual sharing of data, practitioners built knowledge together, across and within programs. The community was an important audience in all stages of the research project, from inception, through data collection and analysis, to writing and dissemination.

One member of the ALPIP community, for example, was a curriculum developer at a community-based literacy and job readiness agency for women. Her program emphasized participatory, learner-centered pedagogy and was in the process of restructuring for a more participatory administration. At the time she was identifying her inquiry question, the agency was working on how to involve learners in program management and decision making and how best to develop learner leadership in the agency. Philosophically, she also had a strong belief in the importance of making agency and classroom work as participatory as possible and in facilitating learner leadership. In this context, she wrote: "Because [the agency] is in the middle of this restructuring process, it seemed to be a particularly timely and useful area for my research. . . . I realized that I might be assuming some definitions of learner leadership that others in the agency may not share and that this would be a good place to start" (Haff, 1993, p. 2).

What is clear is her intent that the inquiry inform both her and her colleagues about issues vital to the life of the agency. Her question, initially framed as "What is learner leadership at my program?" was later expanded with additional questions: "How has it looked in the past?" "How could it look in the future?" Embedded within these specific questions, however, are a number of more general questions, relevant to the wider community as well as her agency: What difference does it make for learners to be involved in leadership roles in adult literacy programs? What is the relationship between leadership experience and learners' ability to meet their literacy or other goals? How can learners be more involved in a variety of program aspects? What are some of the challenges in involving learners in leadership roles? Many literacy programs and practitioners in her seminar and elsewhere struggle with questions about learner leadership and making programs more participatory, so her project can also contribute to ongoing, more public conversation.

Because many agree that generic solutions to problems in adult literacy are inadequate for the situated nature of the work and the different constraints that operate in different settings, building inquiry communities that have the potential to redefine practitioners' relationships to knowledge seems extremely critical. What has been increasingly evident in this work is that practitioner research enfranchises teachers, tutors, and administrators as knowledge makers. Practitioners' questions in the ALPIP project raised issues about the critical and epistemological aspects of practice. They addressed issues of race, class, and gender. All involved seem to be seeking to alter aspects of the existing structures and power relationships by examining such issues as which texts are taught; how teachers, administrators, and learners share power; and the extent to which program management and leadership represent participatory processes.

In forming and building the inquiry community, participants took a critical stance. They questioned common practice, deliberated about what they regarded as expert knowledge, examined underlying assumptions, and attempted to unpack the arrangements and structures of adult literacy education to understand their sources and impacts. In addition, each of their individual projects had the potential to stimulate some form of change, first through its implementation and dissemination on site and second through the seminar as a collaborative community. The participants' collective work suggests that these kinds of practitioner inquiry communities regard educational problems and issues not solely as individual matters but also as social, cultural, and political concerns that may require collective action.

Taking an Inquiry Stance: Corollaries and Consequences

One of the ALPIP seminar participants wrote in her midyear portfolio reflection: "The seminar has made me more critical of my own practice, more apt to make my assumptions about teaching and learning explicit and conscious. If I had not been in this seminar I believe that I would be much less uncertain about my teaching. I don't see my uncertainty as a drawback, but rather as a stage of my growth and development. . . . Essentially, the seminar has caused me to question almost everything I do in the classroom. It is a wonderfully terrible place to be" (Harrill).

For the teachers and administrators in this community, *taking an inquiry stance* is both the process and the most significant outcome of this opportunity for professional development. Their work shows knowledge construction from and for the field through practitioner inquiry and some of the ways that practice is informed by this knowledge. There is considerable evidence here that systematic and intentional inquiry into practice is both essential to and constitutive of meaningful change. Such change contributes to altering practitioners' relationships to knowledge, practice, and agency. The following are some conclusions drawn from the ALPIP project, juxtaposed with excerpts from interviews with participating teachers and administrators.

Knowledge. • Participants came to see their practice as rich sites for learning; they positioned themselves self-consciously as learners from the daily exigencies of their work in programs:

> By systematically investigating the relationships between tutors' beliefs and successful tutoring, I was able to pay close attention to the specific attitudes, knowledge, and expectations that tutors bring into the literacy program and the impact this has on successful tutoring. This understanding can and will generate new dialogue between tutors, students, and myself. [Drucker]

• Participants positioned themselves as knowledge generators by posing and addressing their own questions and interests. They saw this process as having important parallels to curriculum and instruction in learner-centered classrooms and programs. In addition, they repositioned themselves vis-à-vis learners as sources of knowledge for teaching:

I was discovering new methods of improving my own practice, methods which differed wildly from those that I was taught in graduate school. . . . Although I was skeptical and reluctant, the ALPIP inquiry methods that I first thought were "flaky" and "politically correct" began to revolutionize my teaching practice. The validation of my experience and knowledge and the learning of tools that I could use to explore my own questions about teaching were deeply empowering. [Harrill]

- Practitioners came to view research as a systematic and intentional approach to generating local knowledge. They regarded this both as a powerful means to know their own knowledge and as a way to construct knowledge about practice for their communities:

I think that in practice you're a researcher without consciously knowing you're a researcher. You just take information in and you hold it, and if something pops up, you can apply it. If something works in one class well, you think about what made it work well, and you try it in another class. So you're researching what you do all the time. I look at myself in a more credible manner now as a researcher, because [my research is] more structured. [The seminar] offered me the discipline to develop. It provided an arena for me to develop a discipline that I didn't have before, to write more, to reflect more on what I wrote, and if not answer the questions, to have those questions as running questions throughout my practice. [McGovern]

Practice. • For practitioners, reconstructing practice was not primarily about taking on or trying out specific activities and behaviors but rather enriching theories of practice. Framing their practice with what's going on? and what happens when? questions rather than what works? questions represents a significant shift in their stance on the relationships of practice and knowledge:

Before this I'd probably go into class and teach it and go home and not think about it anymore. . . . Now I think about how should I do this? And how did I do this? And I wonder what it means. I have much more of a sense that we're together making some meaning out of this, and that there are fewer rules somehow. [Harrill]

The process of discussion and journal writing in ALPIP has made me more self-reflective about teaching and, I think, more interested and less critical of my teaching. I find myself thinking more often, "Hmm, what's happening here?" rather than, "Oh, shit, I must be doing this wrong." Related to this, I'm more willing to take risks in class. [Gordon]

- Practitioners made their frameworks for teaching more explicit to themselves and more visible in their daily practice. They actively sought opportunities to interrogate these frameworks in collaboration with both learners and colleagues:

As the coordinator of an adult literacy program, I often find it difficult to situate myself within the tutor-student dialogue. This inquiry project instigated a measurement and evaluation process that included tutors' and students' responses to questions, but also, in an important way for me, an evaluation process of myself and my program. The inquiry process helped me to focus on the essentially collaborative and "cooperative enterprise" potential in my program. [Drucker]

Agency. • Practitioners became increasingly committed to the exploration and development of their own practice and more willing to make themselves vulnerable in the context of a community that valued and validated inquiry:

I think that for so many of us in the seminar the idea of having community was really helpful, and yet it's really scary too. I think we're used to classrooms being private. I think that for a lot of people, and certainly it was for me, to bring something from my classroom and say this is what I'm doing was scary. I think that when people do that there's some ego on the line. . . . That's certainly what the fear is. And it's real hard to negotiate that because you want challenge and you want to be pushed past what you're already doing or you wouldn't be there, and yet there's a lot of resistance to that too. [Gordon]

• Through participation in the inquiry community, practitioners diminished the potency of isolation, competition, and hegemonic systems, which had functioned as barriers to influencing policy in the wider field:

Through this group we can make some kind of impact in the field. . . . I don't feel a lot of the policy makers have as much control as I felt they did. . . . I feel, well, if you've got this other voice, maybe they have to listen to it, and I think it's worth getting stronger and more powerful. . . . It's all got to do with isolation and feeling less isolated. I hope that I can do something to have some kind of effect on the larger field. [Fleschute]

Conclusion

Inquiry-based professional and staff development alters the ways participants conceive of their roles as teachers, program leaders, and colleagues. There is considerable evidence that practitioners in these collegial communities actively seek opportunities to include others in similarly rich field-based professional development. Practitioner research into daily practice, beginning as a felt need or tentative question, over time provides the impetus for initiating and sustaining significant change in teaching, curriculum development, assessment, and program organization. Because these learning communities strengthen professional networks, they also support practitioners' leadership efforts beyond the local context, in regional, state, and national arenas. Meaningful change in practice—broadly construed—occurs when field-based practitioners, often in conjunction with learners, have the opportunity to investigate systematically the issues they identify as important.

References

Cochran-Smith, M., and Lytle, S. L. *Inside/Outside: Teacher Research and Knowledge.* New York: Teachers College Press, 1993.

Haff, P. "Learners and Leadership in a Participatory Literacy Program." In S. L. Lytle and E. Cantafio (eds.), *The Inquiries of Adult Literacy Practitioners: Works in Progress.* Unpublished manuscript, 1993.

Lytle, S. L. "Living Literacy: Rethinking Development in Adulthood." *Linguistics and Education,* 1991, 3, 109–138.

Lytle, S. L., and Cochran-Smith, M. "Teacher Research as a Way of Knowing." *Harvard Educational Review,* 1993, 62 (4), 447–474.

McGuire, P. "Constructing Participatory Staff Development." In S. L. Lytle and E. Cantafio (eds.), *The Inquiries of Adult Literacy Practitioners: Works in Progress.* Unpublished manuscript, 1993.

SUSAN L. LYTLE is associate professor in the Graduate School of Education, University of Pennsylvania, and director of the National Center on Adult Literacy at the University of Pennsylvania.

An overview of the perspectives and suggestions presented in this volume indicates some features of a vision for the future of community-based literacy programming.

Reflection as Vision: Prospects for Future Literacy Programming

Peggy A. Sissel

"Reading . . . is the process of constructing meaning through the interaction among a reader's background knowledge, the information suggested by the text, and the context of the reading situation," say Soifer and others (1990, pp. 4–5). They conceptualize the act of reading as much more than the development of skills or mere competency in decoding words, seeing it as a "dynamic interaction" that takes place in concert with a reader's prior knowledge base, life experience, and cultural understandings. It follows that the teaching of reading should also be a dynamic process that not only engages learners with their materials, but learners with learners, learners with teachers, and learners with their community.

The importance of establishing an interactive setting for learning, one that combines context, community, culture, and collaboration, has been the primary theme running through all the preceding chapters. Though each has focused on a different setting or group of learners, the message is the same: the one-size-fits-all programming for low-literate adults that has predominated in the past should not and indeed cannot continue in the future if practitioners are to be responsive to learners' needs. Rather, practitioners must meaningfully assist adults in learning to read not only the word but their world (Freire and Macedo, 1987).

As a means of reflecting on the chapter authors' contributions to a dialogue about the potential and future of literacy programming, this chapter first revisits the issues of context and culture, of creating community and connection in learning settings, and of program participation and collaboration. Then, in light of practitioner concerns, visions, and prescriptions for change, the chapter concludes with some questions for practitioners to consider, a way of

NEW DIRECTIONS FOR ADULT AND CONTINUING EDUCATION, no. 70, Summer 1996 © Jossey-Bass Publishers

reflecting on the dynamics that exist between learners and educators, and a corresponding vision for the future.

Context and Culture

Although the emphasis on individual skill building alone has predominated in the past, it is now understood that the development of literacy skills should not be separated from the content of what is read or from the "social, historical, political, cultural, and personal situations in which people use their skills" (Fingeret, 1992, p. 3). Rather, as Fingeret emphasizes, "effective literacy providers work with adult learners to help them use their life experience as a positive foundation for continuing to learn" (p. 5).

If the learner is to incorporate life experience into his or her learning, practitioners must understand the learner's world and life experience, both as an individual and as a member of his or her cultural group or community. The chapters in this volume provide many insights for practitioners to consider in this area. Cuban and Hayes's chapter emphasizes the neglected needs of women in family literacy programs, suggesting how a gender-based analysis can initiate new ways of thinking about future programming for this population. Peterson's historical perspective on African Americans' experiences with literacy programming reminds us that the cumulative past of a people in relation to education, racism, and poverty has a profound influence on their view of the value of certain types of learning and the types of opportunities and experiences they may have access to. Velázquez further expounds on this reality as it relates to migrant farmworkers, analyzing the way in which ethnicity, geography, and lifestyle intersect and shape people's rejecting of or coping with educational systems. In their chapter on prison literacy programs, James, Witte, and Tal-Mason also visit this theme of the intersecting forces of education, lifestyle, and setting on learners' experience and outlook.

Yet, as Giroux (1987) points out, familiarizing oneself with learner history and experiences is for naught unless one uses this information to help learners acquire their own understanding of their experience with literacy in relation to their world. Essential to this emerging understanding is the creation of a learning setting that promotes both dialogue and a sense of community among learners. Educating through context and culture, therefore, is an essential component of the future of literacy programming.

Community and Connection

Many scholars and practitioners have begun to appreciate the impact that the development of community and connection can have on learners. Scholarship in the area of feminist pedagogy and adult education has emphasized the power and importance of the social role of connection in educational settings, not only among learners but between teachers and learners (Belenky, Clinchy, Goldberger, and Tarule, 1986; Hayes, 1989). Kazemek (1988), Jurmo (1989), and Gowen (1992) have all argued that programs must be more supportive of learners' need to communicate and connect with each other. Quigley's experimental study (1993) showed the importance of personal connection as it relates to persistence and reduced attrition levels, and most recently, my work (Sissel, 1995) on learning among Head Start parents also supports the importance of helping learners acquire supportive connections, connections that then foster learning.

As Candy (1991) has noted, "learning in its fullest context is a social activity" (p. 22), an insight addressed by all the contributors. In their chapter, for example, Bingman, Martin, and Trawick recount employing the social realities of their learners' community as a source of information and a means of helping learners make connections to each other. Cuban and Hayes emphasize the need for women to hear each other's stories as a means of dispelling the isolation that many women feel upon entering programs. Beder's chapter on popular education, viewing community in yet another but equally compelling way, illustrates how popular education helps learners make connections to their world through their activity in a community of committed learners.

Participation

Whether or not a sense of community in the learning setting is created with and among learners and teachers is dependent upon the social dynamics that exist between them. Although social relations between adult educators and learners may appear to be an apolitical phenomenon, the way in which educators speak with and of learners, their modes of interacting with learners, and the choices that they make about the act of teaching—when they act either *on* or *with* learners—are related to issues of power, privilege, and personal politics (Rist, 1970; Giroux, 1981; Tisdell, 1993; Ginsburg, Kamat, Raghu, and Weaver, 1995). These conscious and unconscious, overt and covert behaviors may promote or discourage participation and involvement. And they are reflected in the designing, planning, structuring, and promoting of programs with messages, models, and means that stress either the inclusion or exclusion of certain populations of learners, thereby encouraging or inhibiting them from enrolling and attending.

All these factors then lay the foundation for either promoting or impeding the creation of a meaningful partnership between educators and learners. The authors in this volume have stated that programming that promotes partnership is learner centered and participatory, allowing learners to have a voice in planning activities and agendas. In meaningful partnerships, learners make decisions about the possible outcomes of learning, play a role in selecting the resources to be employed, and play a role in the assessment of their own learning (Lytle, Belzer, Schultz, and Vannozzi, 1989; Fingeret, 1992).

The research on participatory learning and the need for an understanding of the power dynamics and program issues that it involves (Fingeret and Jurmo, 1989) underscore the importance of self-reflection on the part of adult educators.

Inquiry and Reflection

The role of reflection in practice has its roots in the work of Freire (1970) and has since been elaborated on by Schön (1990), Brookfield (1995), and others. In Susan Lytle's chapter on the use of systematic inquiry, she describes the importance of the act of reflection to the practitioner not only as an individual engaging in practice but also as one consciously seeking to become a member of a learning community committed to the process of professional growth and development through active engagement and inquiry.

All the contributors to this volume allude to the vital role that such introspection can play in practice. Lytle, Beder, Hohn and Sissel, and others also point out that this questioning by practitioners must lead to action, for the mere questioning of the issues of context and culture of low-literate adults can too often lead to paternalism or even victim blaming. The creation of community and the promotion of participation with learners require concrete steps, not just the acquisition of knowledge about learners. Questioning and reflection are but the first steps toward the transformation of literacy programs into "learning organizations" (Watkins and Marsick, 1993) that can be increasingly responsive to the needs of learners.

Inherent in this transformation is a new attitude about staff development. Foster (1990) and Fingeret (1992) have pointed out the problems with staff development in literacy programming that affect student retention and outcomes. Therefore, it is clear that staff development practices must be critiqued, as part of our recognition that "status quo" (Fingeret, 1990) literacy programming has not yet ameliorated the "literacy problem" and is unlikely to do so in the future (Chisman, 1990; Foster, 1990).

To achieve the instructional programming that focuses on context and community for learners, staff development must move away from the old individualized, decontextualized model and focus. Instead, staff development must help staff learn to create dynamic interactions among students, between students and teachers, and between teachers. This begins with the recognition of the interconnectedness of three key components: information about the reality of learners' lived experience, accurate appraisal of teachers' current practice, and critical recognition of teachers' need for personal and professional growth and development. Lytle's chapter contains powerful reminders to practitioners that although the act of reflection can be individual, it is only through systematic inquiry and the making of connections within a community that the required changes in literacy education can take place.

Framing the Future

The authors in this sourcebook have suggested various ways of questioning and envisioning the future of literacy programming. In addition to the questions for reflection put forward by Lytle, Hohn and Sissel, and Beder, the following questions may guide practitioners' inquiry.

What does the face of low literacy look like in my community?
What are the sociocultural and contextual backgrounds of my learners?
What can I (we) learn from them?
How can I (we) learn it?
What program aspects are incompatible with learners' needs?
What should the future of literacy programming look like in my community?
What more do I (we) need to learn in order to implement that vision?
What resources do I (we) need?
What types of partnerships need to be developed?
How can I create connections among learners?
How can I (we) go about building a community among learners? Among program staff? Among programs?

Conclusion

The way in which we view learners' difference or sameness from ourselves and the levels and types of informational, cultural, and interpersonal resources they bring to the setting can profoundly affect our expectations about their potential to be involved in the planning of their learning, our expectations about their abilities to do well, and our expectations about their capacity to contribute to and cooperate in their own assessment (Sissel, 1994, 1995).

Therefore, in addition to our reflection on the context of learners' lives and the ways in which knowledge regarding learners' lived experience can shape our practice, we must undertake self-reflection about our vision for the future of literacy programming. We must examine the understanding and assumptions we as practitioners hold about learners in literacy programs and about our role as educators in potential partnership with them (Amstutz, 1994; Flannery, 1994). Honest attempts at coming to grips with our possible prejudices regarding learners and the resulting expectations that we hold about them are an essential foundation to all future action, because such expectations powerfully influence the amount of time, energy, and interest, and the level of resources that we as policy makers, program developers, and educators are willing to invest in learners (Good and Brophy, 1971; U.S. Commission on Civil Rights, 1973; Rist, 1972; Rubovits and Maehr, 1973; Hayes and Colin, 1993; Sissel, 1994, 1995).

The social relations that we have with our learners and colleagues and within our programs may be powerful influences on our view of the potential of low-literate adults. Because of the interactive nature of the resources and expectations that educators and students bring to the social setting and because of the way this dynamic affects programming and practice decisions and participation and involvement, our willingness to reflect upon the way in which we see our learners and our current capacity for creating meaningful learning experiences is essential.

"The new literacy programs must be largely based on the notion of emancipatory literacy, in which literacy is viewed as one of the major vehicles by which oppressed people are able to participate in the sociohistorical transformation of their society" (Freire and Macedo, 1987, p. 157). Women, and people of other colors, ethnicities, classes, and cultures, deserve our highest level of expectations and resources, so that in our programs they can come to see themselves as competent learners who are capable of playing a role in the future of their communities, in the future of their own learning, and in the development of their multiple literacies.

References

Amstutz, D. D. "Staff Development: Addressing Issues of Race and Gender." In E. Hayes and S.A.J. Colin III (eds.), *Confronting Racism and Sexism.* New Directions for Adult and Continuing Education, no. 61. San Francisco: Jossey-Bass, 1994.

Belenky, M. F., Clinchy, B. M., Goldberger, N. R., and Tarule, J. M. *Women's Ways of Knowing: The Development of Self, Voice, and Mind.* New York: Basic Books, 1986.

Brookfield, S. *Becoming a Critically Reflective Teacher.* San Francisco: Jossey-Bass, 1995.

Candy, P. C. *Self-Direction for Lifelong Learning: A Comprehensive Guide to Theory and Practice.* San Francisco: Jossey-Bass, 1991.

Chisman, F. P. "Toward a Literate America: The Leadership Challenge." In F. P. Chisman and Associates, *Leadership for Literacy: The Agenda for the 1990s.* San Francisco: Jossey-Bass, 1990.

Fingeret, A., and Jurmo, P. (eds.). *Participatory Literacy Education.* New Directions for Continuing Education, no. 42. San Francisco: Jossey-Bass, 1989.

Fingeret, H. "Changing Literacy Instruction: Moving Beyond the Status Quo." In F. P. Chisman and Associates, *Leadership for Literacy: The Agenda for the 1990s.* San Francisco: Jossey- Bass, 1990.

Fingeret, H. *Adult Literacy Education: Current and Future Directions—An Update.* ERIC Clearinghouse on Adult, Career, and Vocational Education, Information Series no. 355. Columbus: Center on Education and Training for Employment, College of Education, Ohio State University, 1992.

Flannery, D. D. "Changing Dominant Understandings of Adults as Learners." In E. Hayes and S.A.J. Colin III (eds.), *Confronting Racism and Sexism.* New Directions for Adult and Continuing Education, no. 61. San Francisco: Jossey-Bass, 1994.

Foster, S. E. "Upgrading the Skills of Literacy Professionals: The Profession Matures." In F. P. Chisman and Associates, *Leadership for Literacy: The Agenda for the 1990s.* San Francisco: Jossey Bass, 1990.

Freire, P. *Pedagogy of the Oppressed.* New York: Seabury Press, 1970.

Freire, P., and Macedo, D. *Literacy: Reading the Word and the World.* New York: Bergin & Garvey, 1987.

Ginsburg, M. B., Kamat, S., Raghu, R., and Weaver, J. "Educators and Politics: Interpretations, Involvement, and Implications." In M. B. Ginsburg (ed.), *The Politics of Educators' Work and Lives.* New York: Garland, 1995.

Giroux, H. A. "Teacher Education and the Ideology of Social Control." In H. A. Giroux (ed.), *Ideology, Culture, and the Process of Schooling.* Philadelphia: Temple University Press, 1981.

Giroux, H. A. "Introduction: Literacy and the Pedagogy of Political Empowerment." In P. Freire and D. Macedo, *Literacy: Reading the Word and the World.* New York: Bergin & Garvey, 1987.

Good, T. L., and Brophy, J. E. "Analyzing Classroom Interaction: A More Powerful Alternative." *Educational Technology,* 1971, *11,* 36–41.

Gowen, S. G. *The Politics of Workplace Literacy: A Case Study.* New York: Teachers College Press, 1992.

Hayes, E. "Insights from Women's Experiences for Teaching and Learning." In E. Hayes (ed.), *Effective Teaching Styles*. New Directions for Continuing Education, no. 43. San Francisco: Jossey-Bass, 1989.

Hayes, E., and Colin, S.A.J., III (eds). *Confronting Racism and Sexism*. New Directions for Adult and Continuing Education, no. 61. San Francisco: Jossey-Bass, 1993.

Jurmo, P. "The Case for Participatory Literacy Education." In A. Fingeret and P. Jurmo (eds.), *Participatory Literacy Education*. New Directions for Continuing Education, no. 42. San Francisco: Jossey-Bass, 1989.

Kazemek, F. E. "Women and Adult Literacy: Considering the Other Half of the House." *Lifelong Learning*, 1988, *11* (4), 15, 23–24.

Lytle, S. L., Belzer, A., Schultz, K., and Vannozzi, M. "Learner-Centered Literacy Assessment: An Evolving Process." In A. Fingeret and P. Jurmo (eds.), *Participatory Literacy Education*. New Directions for Continuing Education, no. 42. San Francisco: Jossey-Bass, 1989.

Quigley, A. B. "Curbing Attrition in ABE in the First Three Critical Weeks." Paper presented at the American Association for Adult and Continuing Education conference, Dallas, Tex., Nov. 1993.

Rist, R. C. "Student Social Class and Teacher Expectations: The Self-Fulfilling Prophecy in Ghetto Education." *Harvard Educational Review*, 1970, *40*, 411–451.

Rist, R. C. "Social Distance and Social Inequality in a Ghetto Kindergarten Classroom." *Urban Education*, 1972, *7*, 241–260.

Rubovits, P. C., and Maehr, M. L. "Pygmalion Black and White." *Journal of Personality and Social Psychology*, 1973, *25* (2), 210–218.

Schön, D. A. *Educating the Reflective Practitioner: Toward a New Design for Teaching and Learning in the Professions*. San Francisco: Jossey-Bass, 1990.

Sissel, P. A. "Parents, Learning, and Project Head Start: A Socio-Political Analysis." Paper presented at the 34th annual Adult Education Research conference, Knoxville, Tenn., May 1994.

Sissel, P. A. "Capacity, Power, and Connection: An Ethnographic Study of Parents, Learning, and Project Head Start." Unpublished doctoral dissertation, Graduate School of Education, Rutgers, the State University of New Jersey, 1995.

Soifer, R., Irwin, M. E., Crumrine, B. M., Honzaki, E., Simmons, B. K., and Young, D. L. *The Complete Theory-to-Practice Handbook of Adult Literacy: Curriculum Design and Teaching Approaches*. New York: Teachers College Press, 1990.

Tisdell, E. J. "Interlocking Systems of Power, Privilege, and Oppression in Adult Higher Education Classes." *Adult Education Quarterly*, 1993, *43* (4), 203–226.

U.S. Commission on Civil Rights. *Teachers and Students: Differences in Teacher Interaction with Mexican American and Anglo Students*. Report V: *Mexican American Education Study*. Washington, D.C.: U.S. Government Printing Office, 1973.

Watkins, K. E., and Marsick, V. J. *Sculpting the Learning Organization: Lessons in the Art and Science of Systemic Change*. San Francisco: Jossey-Bass, 1993.

PEGGY A. SISSEL is assistant professor, Center for Research on Teaching and Learning, College of Education, University of Arkansas at Little Rock, and adjunct assistant professor, Department of Pediatrics, University of Arkansas for Medical Sciences.

INDEX

ORDERING INFORMATION

NEW DIRECTIONS FOR ADULT AND CONTINUING EDUCATION is a series of paperback books that explores issues of common interest to instructors, administrators, counselors, and policy makers in a broad range of adult and continuing education settings—such as colleges and universities, extension programs, businesses, the military, prisons, libraries, and museums. Books in the series are published quarterly in Spring, Summer, Fall, and Winter and are available for purchase by subscription and individually.

SUBSCRIPTIONS for 1996 cost $50.00 for individuals (a savings of 34 percent over single-copy prices) and $72.00 for institutions, agencies, and libraries. Standing orders are accepted. New York residents, add local sales tax for subscriptions. (For subscriptions outside the United States, add $7.00 for shipping via surface mail or $25.00 for air mail. Orders *must be prepaid* in U.S. dollars by check drawn on a U.S. bank or charged to VISA, MasterCard, or American Express.)

SINGLE COPIES cost $19.00 plus shipping (see below) when payment accompanies order. California, New Jersey, New York, and Washington, D.C., residents, please include appropriate sales tax. Canadian residents, add GST and any local taxes. Billed orders will be charged shipping and handling. No billed shipments to post office boxes. (Orders from outside the United States *must be prepaid* in U.S. dollars by check drawn on a U.S. bank or charged to VISA, MasterCard, or American Express.)

SHIPPING (SINGLE COPIES ONLY): one issue, add $5.00; two issues, add $6.00; three issues, add $7.00; four to five issues, add $8.00; six to seven issues, add $9.00; eight or more issues, add $12.00.

DISCOUNTS FOR QUANTITY ORDERS are available. Please write to the address below for information.

ALL ORDERS must include either the name of an individual or an official purchase order number. Please submit your order as follows:
    Subscriptions: specify series and year subscription is to begin
    Single copies: include individual title code (such as ACE 59)

MAIL ALL ORDERS TO:
    Jossey-Bass Publishers
    350 Sansome Street
    San Francisco, California 94104-1342

FOR SUBSCRIPTION SALES OUTSIDE OF THE UNITED STATES, contact any international subscription agency or Jossey-Bass directly.

OTHER TITLES AVAILABLE IN THE
NEW DIRECTIONS FOR ADULT AND CONTINUING EDUCATION SERIES
Ralph G. Brockett, Susan Imel, Editors-in-Chief
Alan B. Knox, Consulting Editor